SECRET GATESHEAD

Rob Kirkup

T0307514

AMBERLEY

In loving memory of my mam

First published 2017

Amberley Publishing
The Hill, Stroud
Gloucestershire, GL5 4EP

www.amberley-books.com

ISBN 978 1 4456 6638 9 (print)
ISBN 978 1 4456 6639 6 (ebook)

British Library Cataloguing in Publication Data.
A catalogue record for this book is available from the British Library.

Origination by Amberley Publishing.
Printed in Great Britain.

Contents

Introduction

I have lived all my life on the northern side of the Tyne, growing up in a small village called Annitsford, not far from Cramlington, and these days I live in Wallsend. Despite not having ever been able to call Gateshead home, I've always had a close affinity for the town as my mam was born and raised in Wrekenton, and her side of the family still lives in and around the area to this day. There are connections on my dad's side of the family too, as I have fond memories of being a child and jumping in the car every Christmas Day with my parents, my brother and my nana, clutching my favourite toy from Santa and going to see Aunty Mary (Dad's sister), Uncle Steve, and my cousins Sharon and Glyn at their house in Winlaton.

Over the decades I've looked on in wonder at the evolution that the town of Gateshead has undergone, which has been so drastic and rapid that it's been almost impossible to ignore. I grew up in the 1980s and didn't understand the hardship that was being felt by the people of Gateshead. The previous decade had seen many of the town's traditional industries decline. As the majority of people living there worked in these industries, it lead to huge unemployment. What I saw was the Great North Run, with the first-ever race being ran in 1981 and being beamed live all over the world, putting Gateshead on the map.

The MetroCentre opened its doors on 15 October 1986 – the largest shopping centre in all of Europe – and I can remember the first time I walked in its doors as a wide-eyed child full of wonder and astonishment. This shopping centre was unlike anything I'd ever seen; I felt like I'd found a golden ticket in my Marathon chocolate bar and won a trip around Willy Wonka's Chocolate Factory. There were toyshops everywhere, including an enormous Toys R Us, and there was even an amusement park inside with a rollercoaster.

The regeneration that has happened since with Trinity Square, the Angel of the North, St Mary's Heritage Centre, Bottle Bank, and of course the breathtaking sight that is the Gateshead Quays has brought Gateshead into the twenty-first century with a real bang and, having applied for city status in 2012 as part of the Queen's jubilee celebrations, it can only be a matter of time before it is officially named a city.

Within this book I will look at some of the lesser-known aspects of this great town – from the beginning of Gateshead, or Goat's Head, through to this very day. Along the way I will introduce you to some of the residents who've made a real difference in the world of sport, music (even dating the Earth) who all deserve to be far better known that they are. We will explore some of its haunted houses, ghoulish graveyards, and visit the church where the dead body of an alien was hidden after it was killed by an angry Geordie in wartime Gateshead. We will also look at the impact of two world wars on the town, and the town's history of crime and punishment.

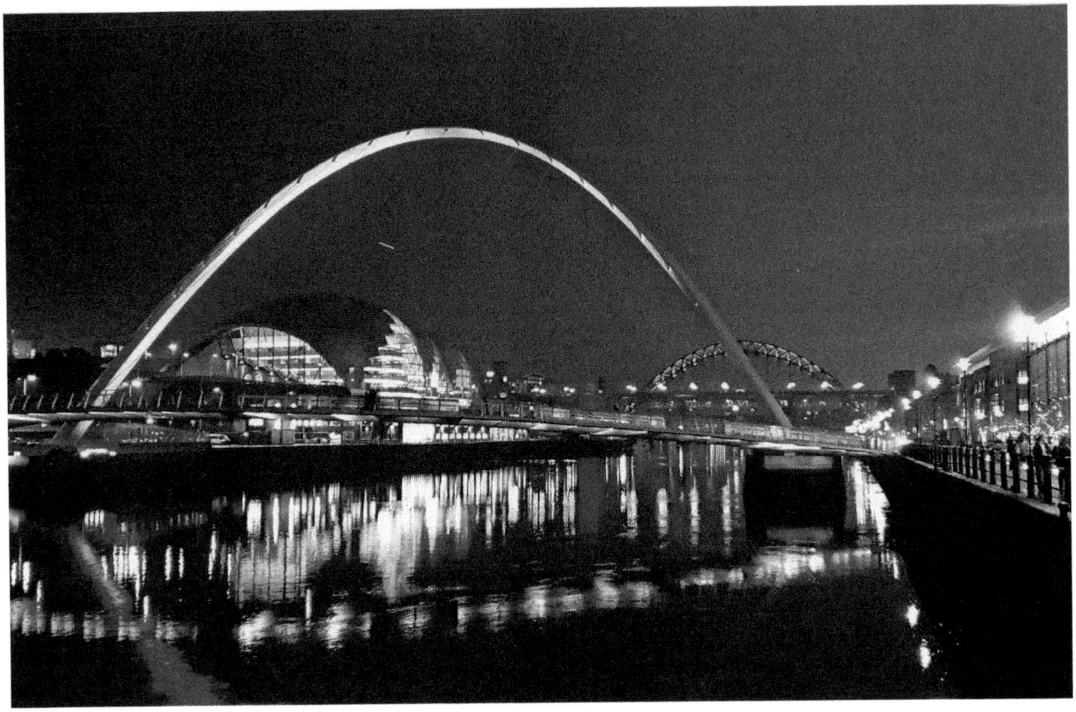

Gateshead Quays at night.

Newcastle is well known in TV and film, but Gateshead is less so – which Gateshead landmarks have made it onto the big screen and the smaller screen? We'll look at all of this and more in *Secret Gateshead.*

1. Beginnings

In contrast with the town's neighbours across the River Tyne, the beginnings of Gateshead are far more difficult to piece together. We know that there was the Roman fort of Port Aelius at Newcastle, which occupied a strategic site protecting a bridge over the Tyne at the site of the current Swing Bridge. An urn containing Roman coins was found in Church Street in 1790, and coins found during roadworks on Bottle Bank in 1802 led to the theory that there may well have been a small settlement on the Gateshead side of the Roman bridge across the Tyne. It would most likely have been on the strategic site now occupied by St Mary's Church – to mirror what was happening on the other side of the river. However, these chance finds in themselves were not confirmation that this was the case.

Concrete evidence of a Roman settlement in Gateshead didn't arrive until almost two centuries later when, between 1994 and 1997, stratified Roman deposits were found during work being carried out to properties near Bottle Bank – at the site the current Hilton Hotel now occupies. Further investigation revealed a section of roadway, stone buildings, ditches and stone-lined cisterns. Remains of pottery point to a date of occupation from the early second century into the fourth century. Historians speculate that this settlement

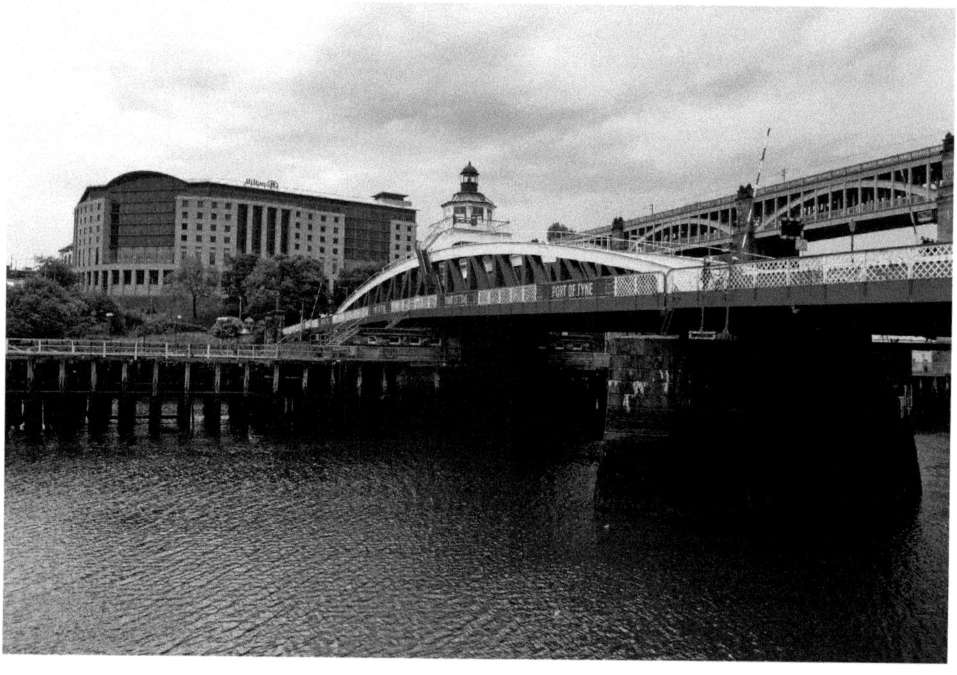

The Swing Bridge with the Hilton Hotel visible behind.

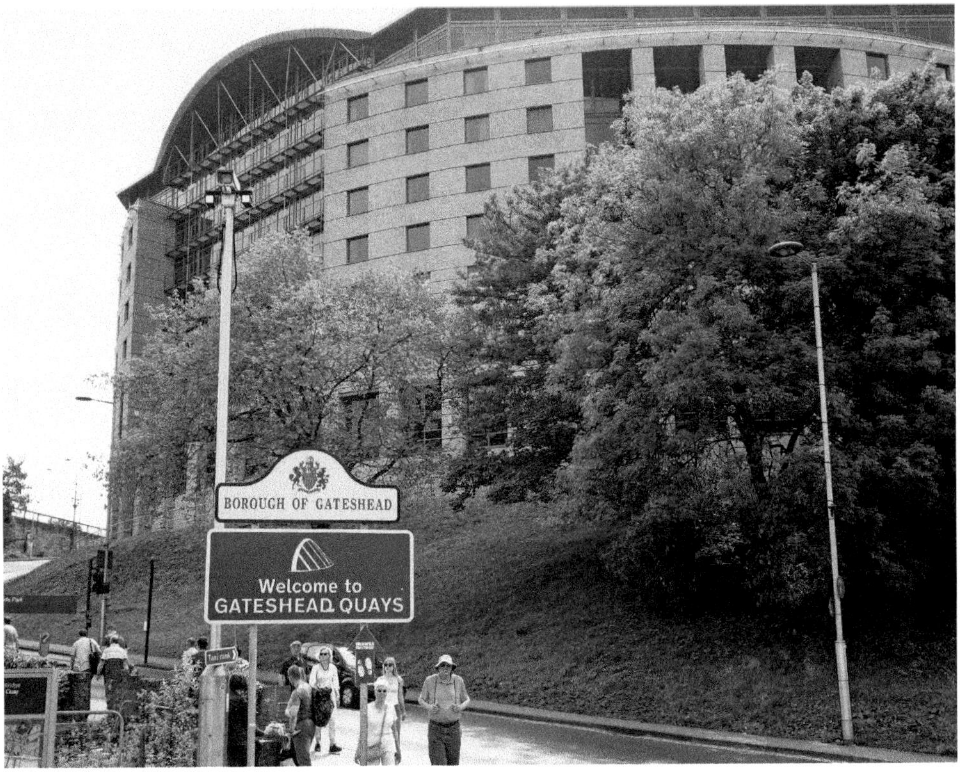

The Hilton Hotel was built on the site of a Roman settlement.

most likely consisted of a row of shops and temples lining the Roman road, capitalising on the trade offered by passing soldiers.

It has also been suggested that Port Aelius was built on the north of the Tyne to replace an earlier fort on the southern side, likely on the site of the current St Mary's Church. An eighteenth-century local historian speculated that some of the oldest stones resemble the Roman style and could have been reclaimed from the remains of a Roman building, possibly from a nearby fort. However, there's no historical evidence to prove that a fort ever existed on the south side of the river. The only confirmed discovery of a Roman fort in Gateshead happened in 1970, when an aerial photograph of a field of crops revealed a fort between Dunston Hill and Whickham. Its close proximity to Washington Farm has led to it being known as Washingwell Fort, as its actual Roman name has been lost to time.

DID YOU KNOW?

When Gateshead FC was formed in 1977 the goat's head was incorporated into the club's badge. This is no longer part of the badge, as it's now the Angel of the North kicking a football.

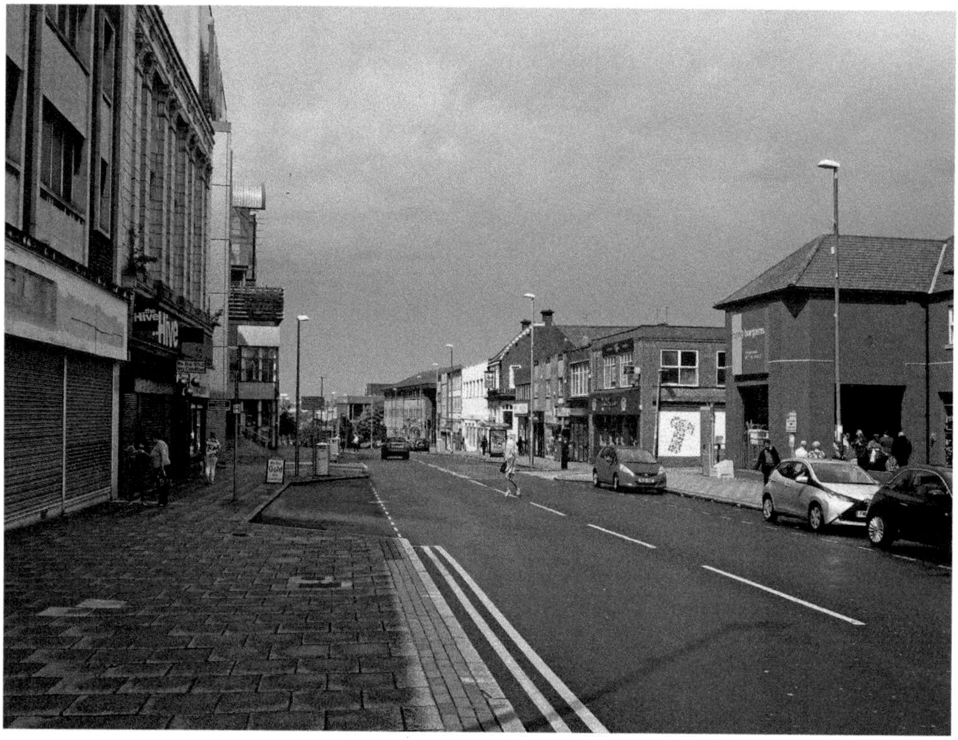

Gateshead High Street, along the route of the Roman Road.

We do know that a Roman road ran from Pons Aelius at Newcastle to the fort of Concangis at Chester-le-Street, which will most have likely passed through Gateshead along the route of the current Gateshead High Street towards what is now Wrekenton, then on to Birtley before reaching the fort at Chester-le-Street. This is part of the Roman road known as Cade's Road – named after John Cade, who proposed its existence in 1785. The course of the road was roughly 100 miles from the Humber Estuary up to the River Tyne. At Wrekenton, Cade's Road met another called the Wekendyke, which ran north-east to the fort of Arbeia at South Shields.

In the year AD 653, the Venerable Bede wrote of a monastery overlooking the bridge across the Tyne, belonging to an abbot called Utta and located on a site in Ad Caprae Caput – this translates to 'Goat's Head'. It has been debated for many years as to whether Bede was writing of Gateshead, but there is evidence to back up that this was the case. There have been suggestions that Gateshead of the day was home to wild goats, while another justification for the name is that there may have been the emblem of a goat's head on the Gateshead side of the Roman bridge. We will likely never know, but what we do know is that eleventh-century English chronicler Symeon of Durham in *History of the Church of Durham* and *Historia Regum* ('History of the Kings') called Saxon Gateshead 'Ad Caput Caprae'.

Despite the town's unclear association to the goat, the symbol of the goat's head has become associated with Gateshead and was incorporated into the town's coat of arms. There have been various iterations of this over the years; until the 1830s a shield

Coat of arms on No. 1 Church Street – the first building on the south side of the Tyne.

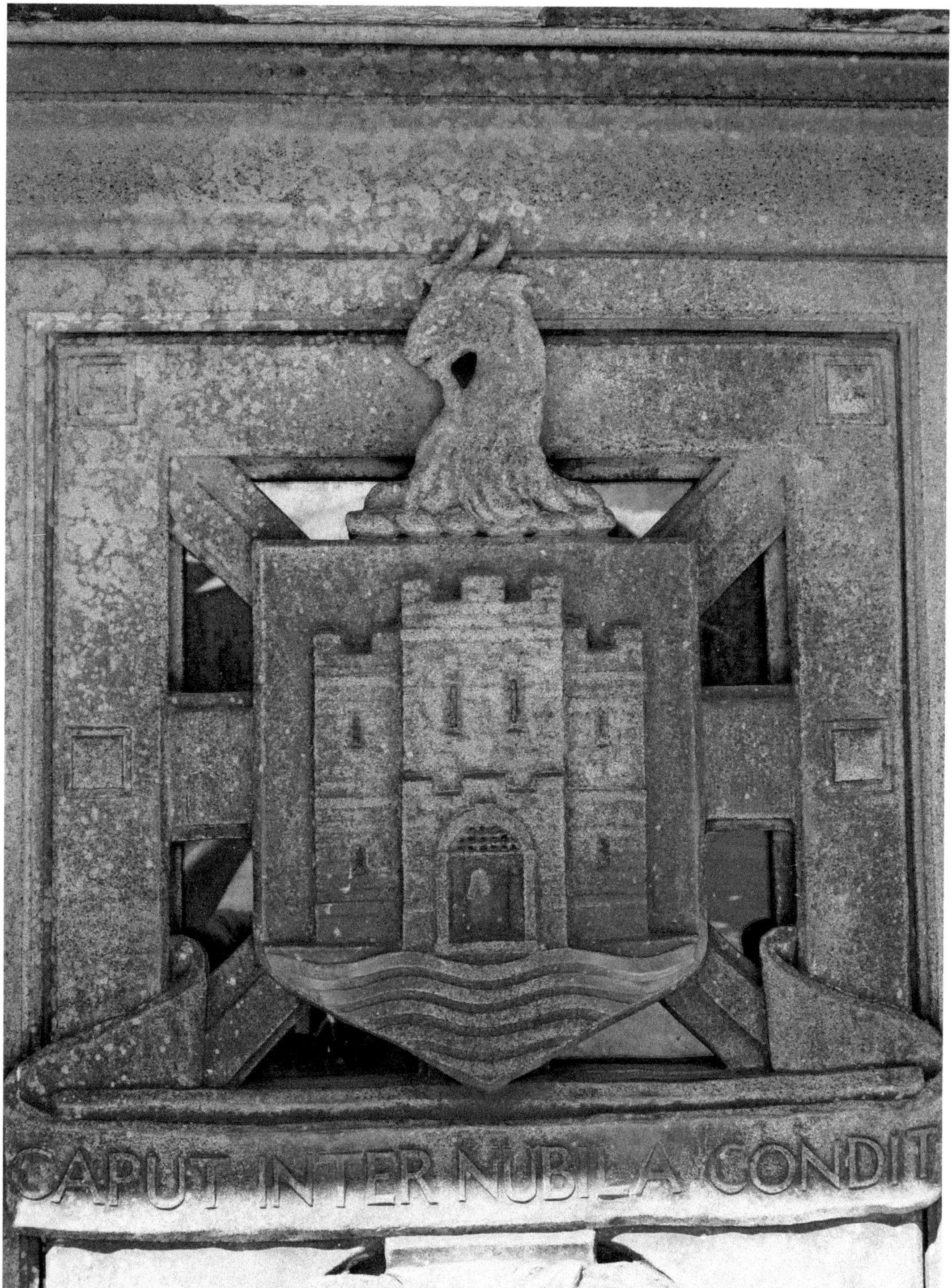

Coat of arms on First World War memorial on Prince Consort Road.

containing a goat's head had another one atop the shield, then the goat's head within the shield was replaced with a gatehouse. During this period a motto was added: '*Caput Inter Nubila Condit*', which is a Latin phrase meaning 'She hides her heads among the clouds'. Around the 1930s a gate necklace was added to the goat, as well as a number of embellishments. With the newly formed Metropolitan Borough of Gateshead in 1974, a new coat of arms was adopted in which the goat no longer features.

Almost nothing is known of Gateshead between AD 653 and 1080, then in 1080 to important events occurred. Following the Norman Conquest, England was ruled by the man who led the invasion, William I – known as William the Conqueror – and his eldest son, Robert Curthose. Having just returned south from leading a large army north to deal with King Malcolm III of Scotland, the king constructed a wooden motte-and-bailey castle on the northern side of the Tyne – the site of the earlier Roman fort. The existing settlement, which was by now called Monkchester, would thrive and grow around this 'new castle', after which it would be named.

The second notable event of 1080 occurred on 14 May, when William Walcher was murdered. Walcher had been appointed as the first-ever Bishop of Durham in 1071 by William I. During a disagreement with some furious Northumbrians he met with a disgruntled crowd at Gateshead. He took refuge in a church there, but when it was set on fire he was forced to leave the burning building and he was slain by the waiting mob.

Eleventh-century Gateshead was referred to as a place rather than a town. It is believed to have been predominantly forest, enclosed by a ditch or hedge and used as a hunting reserve by the bishops of Durham, with other areas of land used for agriculture. In the mid-twelfth century the forest was the subject of Gateshead's first charter, granted by Hugh du Puiset, Bishop of Durham, which set some rules for use of the land by the people of Gateshead. In most parts of England the king would grant charters such as these; however, in places such as Durham – including Gateshead – it was treated as if it was a kingdom within a kingdom with the powerful prince-bishops ruling these lands.

DID YOU KNOW?

In 1539 Gateshead is written as 'Gateshead, near Pipewellgate', and there are recordings of the title of Lord of Pipewellgate being held, leading some to believe that Pipewellgate was once more important than Gateshead.

St Mary's Church, a riverside landmark high above the Tyne, was the only Anglican church in the town until the nineteenth century, leading to it being considered the 'mother church' of Gateshead. It is unknown when the church was originally built, although it's believed the current building dates back to the 1100s, when it had been built on the site of a previous church that was destroyed by fire in 1080.

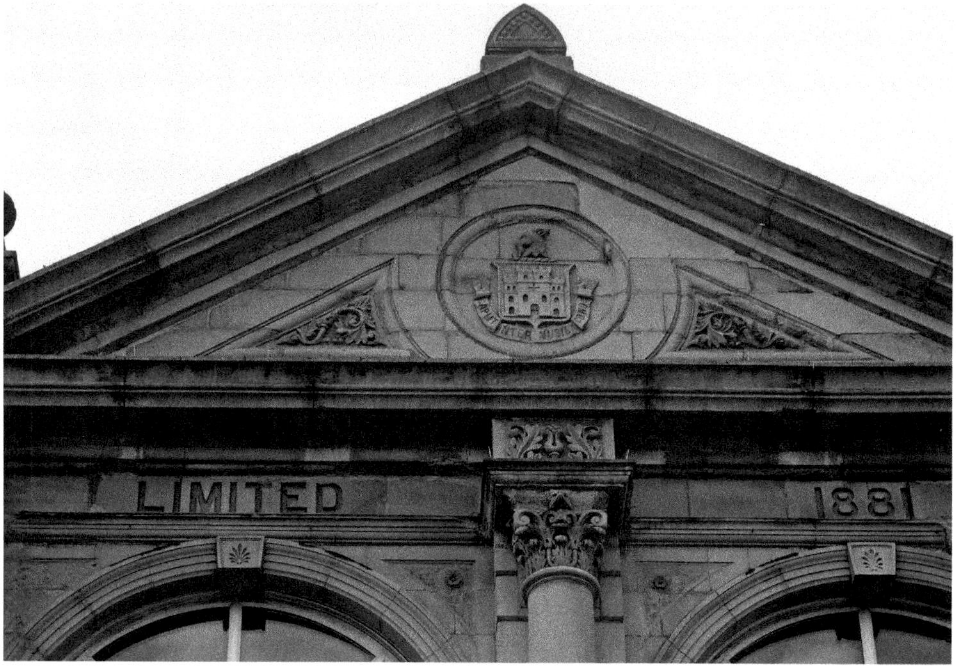

Coat of arms on the Co-op building on Jackson Street.

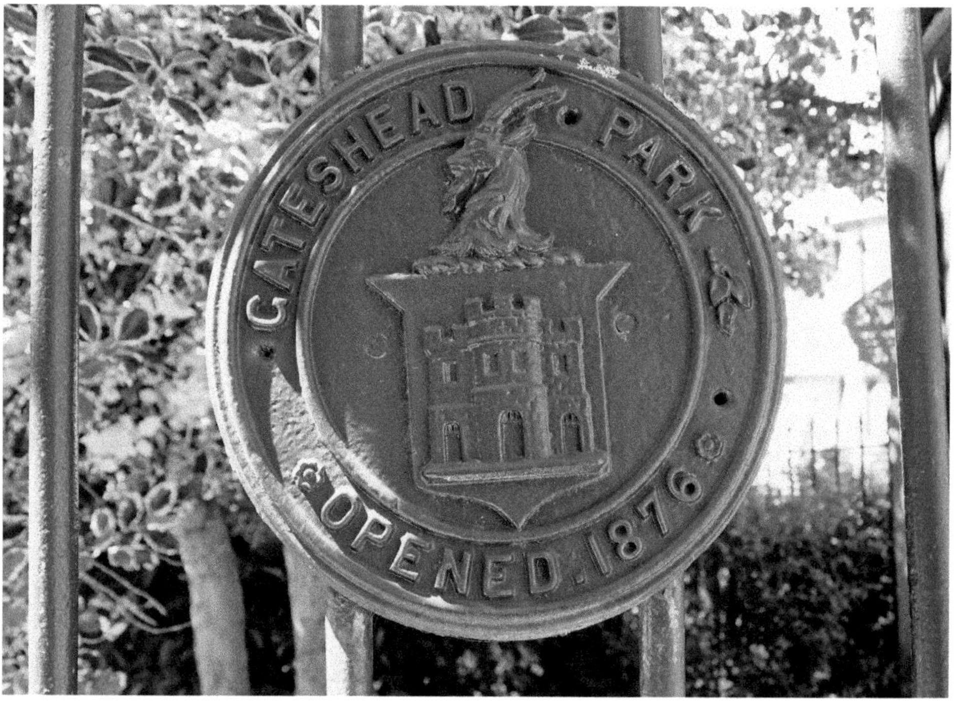

Coat of arms on the gates of Saltwell Park.

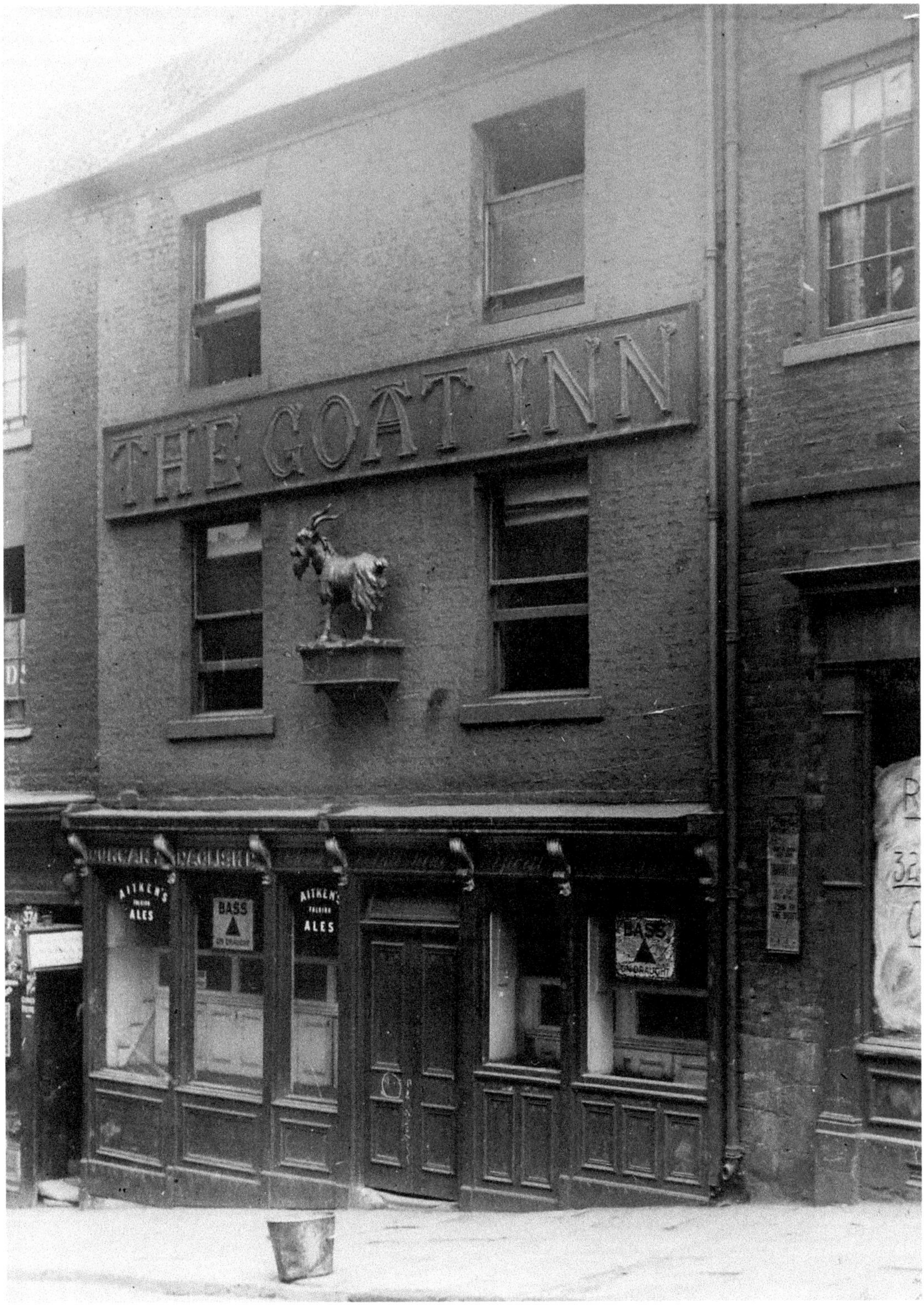

The Goat's Head Inn in 1926. (Photo courtesy of Gateshead Libraries)

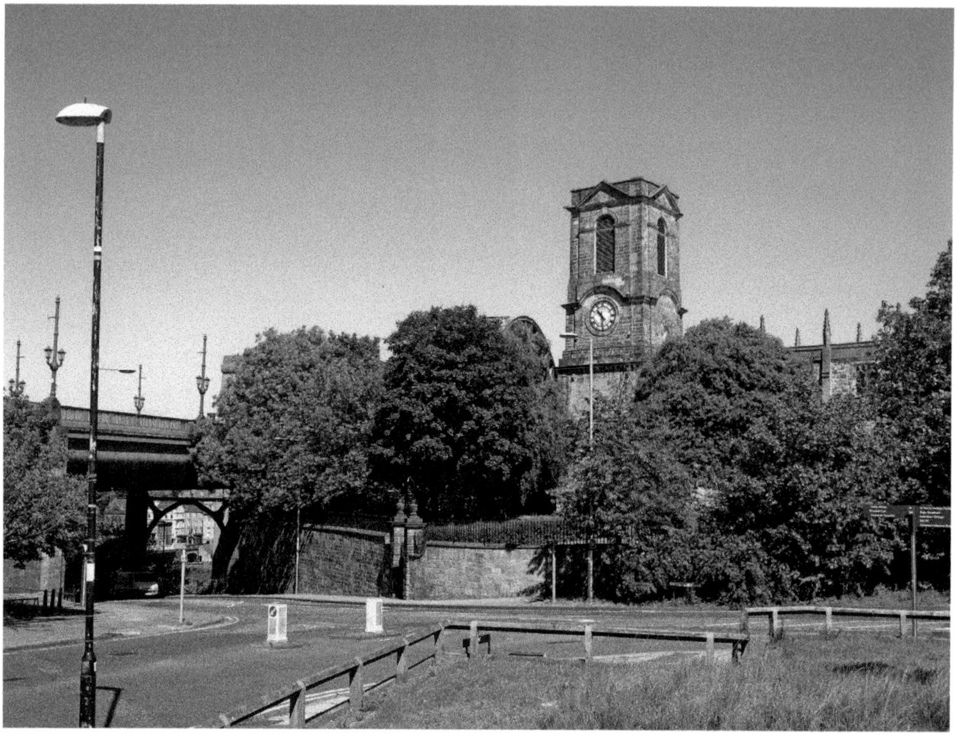

St Mary's Heritage Centre.

In 1183 the Boldon Book was compiled. This was similar to the Domesday Book, which had been created in the previous century, and contained, on the orders of Hugh du Puiset, detail of rents and dues owed to the diocese by the tenants of land under his control. This included most of Durham and also Gateshead. The Boldon Book documents that Gateshead had salmon fisheries, watermills and bakehouses, showing that Gateshead was no longer solely reliant on agriculture. A tax of £10 a year was being paid to the bishop, the highest of any town in Durham.

Gateshead was slowly growing, with the forests gradually being cleared away. Around the end of the twelfth century a chapel existed that doubled as a hospital, and was named for the Holy Trinity. In 1248, the Hospital of St Edmund the Confessor and St Cuthbert was founded. It has been suggested by some that it was built on the previous site on Utta's monastery, which Bede had written off in AD 653. By 1246 a market was being held twice a week – further evidence of Gateshead's progress. The year 1250 saw the building of a new bridge across the River Tyne, an impressive structure with a tower and portcullis on the Gateshead side on the river.

Thirteenth-century Gateshead was small in comparison to Newcastle, with the majority of the housing found along the route of the current High Street and along the riverside streets of Bottle Bank, Hillgate, Oakwellgate and Pipewellgate. Use of the word 'gate' in these street names links to the town being known as Gateshead by this point in time. As late as the 1830s Gateshead had barely expanded beyond this point.

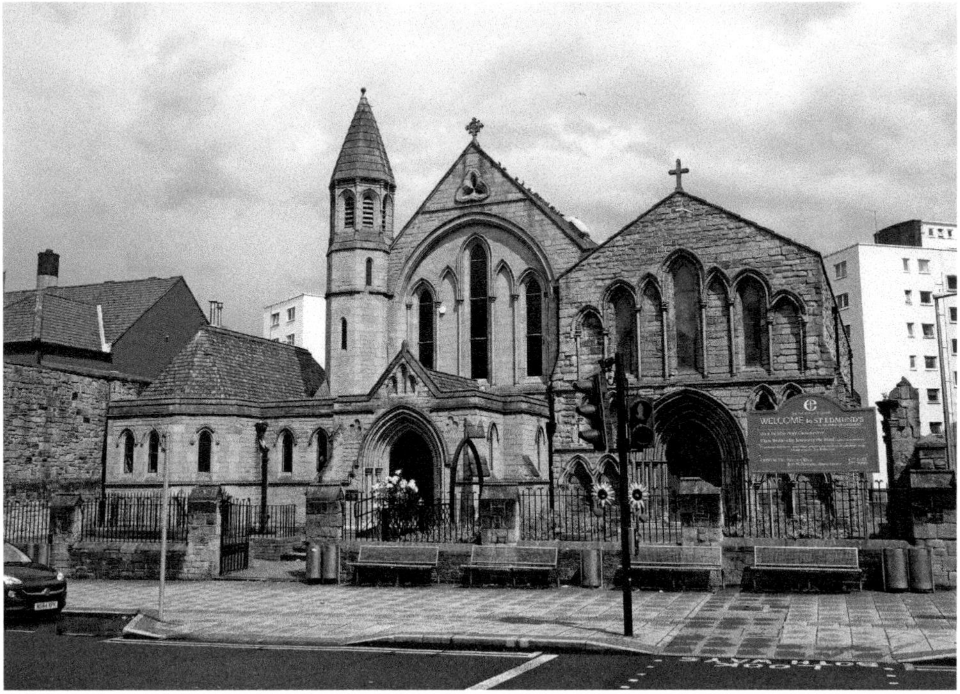

St Edmund's Chapel.

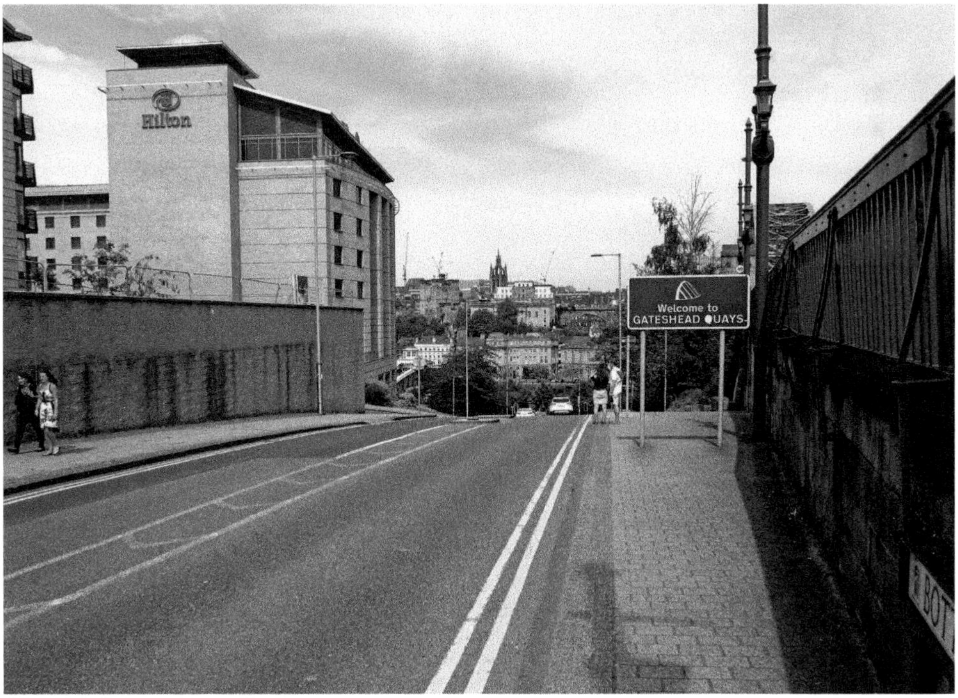

Bottle Bank.

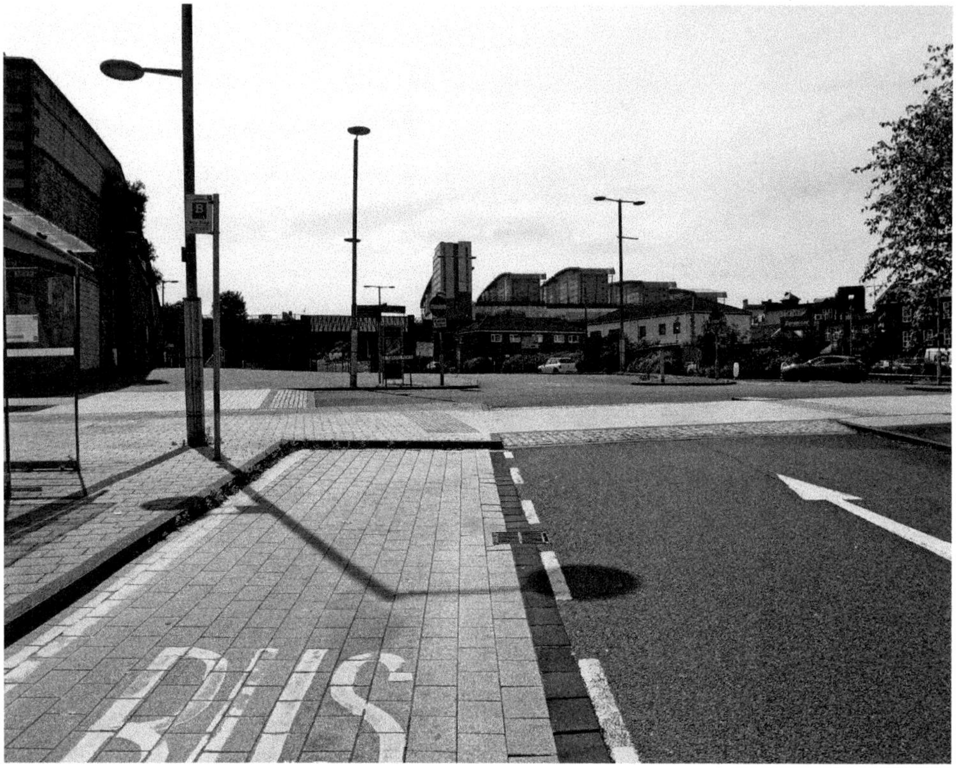

Oakwellgate.

A bailiff was the bishop's representative within the borough of Gateshead and oversaw a small staff, which would include a steward, a sergeant of arrest and four wainmen. Wainmen would collect tolls owed on carts and wagons. The bailiff would then send the revenue onto the bishop. The bailiff was also responsible for holding the borough courts.

As Gateshead's industry along the river thrived, the prince-bishops of Durham struggled to keep hold of the town as the wealthy merchants of Newcastle did their best to take control of it to cash in on the trade on the opposite side of the river. Gateshead merchants and traders were harassed, and the town's fishermen suffered in particular. The fisheries on the south side of the Tyne were destroyed and the catches taken over to Newcastle. In 1334 Edward III had to intervene and, by writ, forbade the mayor and bailiffs of Newcastle to hinder the mooring of ships on the south side of the river.

The southern third of the Tyne Bridge was owned by the Bishop of Durham, but in 1383 the entirety of the bridge was taken over by the city of Newcastle and a tower was constructed on it. However, in 1415 the then bishop, Langley, appealed to the king and the southern part of the bridge (including the newly built tower) was handed back to Gateshead. Gateshead might have won this particular battle, but Newcastle, determined to have sole control of the valuable industry offered by the Tyne, were winning the war. In 1454 Newcastle were granted conservatorship of the river, which gave them a monopoly of its trade for the next 400 years. However, Newcastle wasn't satisfied with this victory, what they truly desired was control of Gateshead's abundance of coal.

The first record of coal mining in Gateshead was in 1344. The town quickly grew a reputation for it, with the mining areas of Gateshead and Wickham considered the best in all of Europe. With Newcastle in control of trade on the Tyne, Richard II granted a charter to the Bishop of Durham in 1384 for the mooring of ships on the river to load and unload coals without molestation from the men of Newcastle. Gateshead's control over these valuable mines would last until 1576, when a small group of Newcastle merchants acquired the 'Grand Lease' of the manors of Gateshead and Wickham.

By 1599, after three centuries of harassment, Gateshead was completely controlled by their much larger neighbour north of the Tyne. It's even recorded that in the early 1600s the bailiffs of Gateshead were appointed by the council of Newcastle, rather than the Bishop of Durham as in previous years.

DID YOU KNOW?

During the thirteenth century the town's name may have been spelt 'Gatishevede', which was found on a legal document from 1430.

During the seventeenth century the population of Gateshead doubled to around 5,500, and coal shipments from Newcastle increased elevenfold. However by the end of the eighteenth century the abundance of coal had begun to run out, as the coal from deeper seams couldn't be accessed due to the threat of flooding and ventilation challenges. The Industrial Revolution saw an explosion in the population of Gateshead, with it growing to over 100,000 during the nineteenth century and seeing the town expand southwards.

In 1854 a catastrophic event happened that would change the face of the town forever. On Friday 6 October the Great Fire of Gateshead saw a series of fires and explosions set ablaze the Gateshead and Newcastle quaysides. Fifty-three people were killed, and it was a miracle there was not more loss of life considering the scale of the devastation. Around 400–500 people were injured, some horribly, and received treatment at the Gateshead Dispensary and Newcastle Infirmary. The damage was incredible, with the entire section of town from the church and Church Walk down to the river, east of Bridge Street (including Hillgate) completely destroyed. The whole of Canon Street, south of St Mary's Church, was ruined. The church itself was saved, but only just, as the fire was extinguished as the flames licked at its ancient stone walls. The houses on Church Walk were demolished as they were damaged beyond repair. On the quayside itself, Singer's Vinegar Factory, the Bond Warehouse, Wilson's Worsted Manufactory, Bulcrauig's Engine Manufactory, and Carr's Timber Yard were all completely destroyed. The extent of buildings consumed by the flames didn't stop there, with a number of tenement housing on the hill overlooking the river destroyed.

From 1835 Gateshead was considered a municipal borough, and then in 1889 it became a county borough, separate from Durham County Council. The Local Government Act of 1972 saw Gateshead become the Metropolitan Borough of Gateshead in 1974, as the County Borough of Gateshead was merged with the urban districts of Ryton, Blaydon, Felling, Whickham and part of Chester-le-Street.

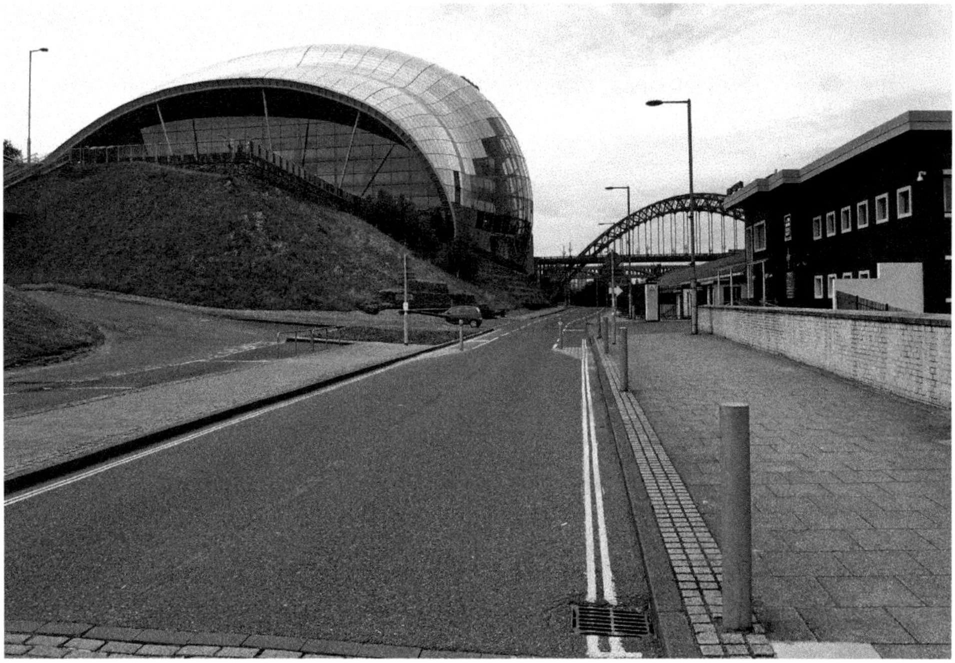

Hillgate.

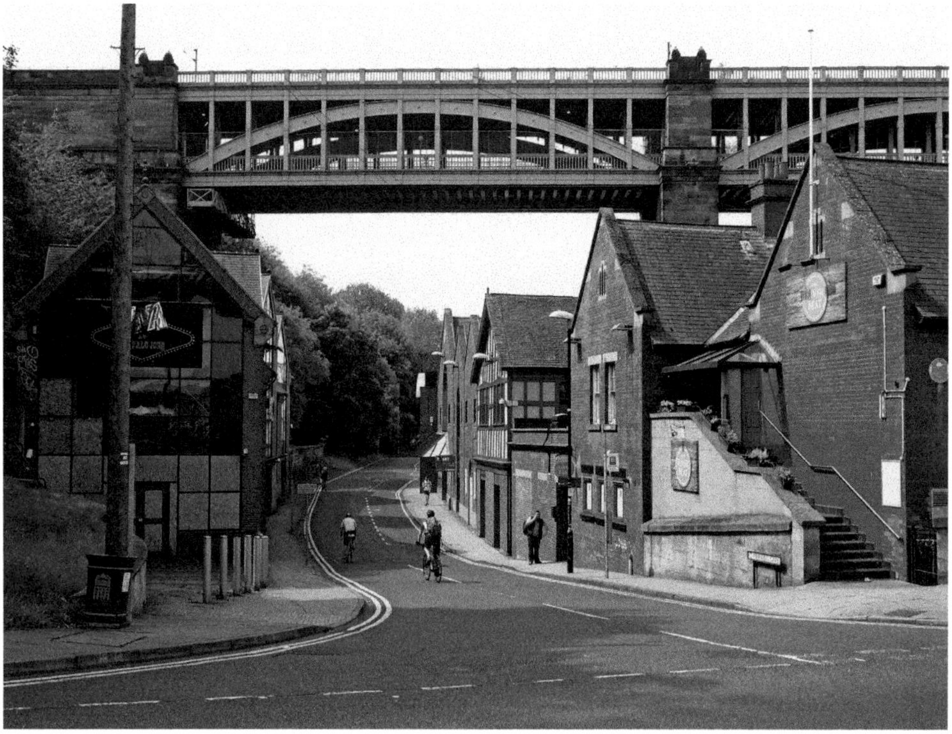

Pipewellgate.

2. Famous Residents

Olympians Steve Cram, Jonathan Edwards and Brendan Foster; the voice of *Big Brother* Marcus Bentley; and AC/DC lead singer Brian Johnson are just some of the famous names to come from Gateshead, but, with this being *Secret Gateshead*, let's look at some of the town's residents past and present that you're less likely to be familiar with.

The people of the north-east are famous for their fevered love of football, and the rivalry between Newcastle and Sunderland is the stuff of legend. So let's begin by looking at a famous footballer born here in Gateshead. We're almost spoilt for choice; we could look at Gateshead-born Andy Carroll, the former Newcastle United striker who became the most expensive British transfer when he joined Liverpool for £35 million in January 2011, or what about Bob Moncur? Born and raised in Scotland, the Scottish international captained Newcastle United to their last major honour when he lifted the Fairs Cup trophy in 1969. Moncur now lives in Low Fell, and was awarded the freedom of Gateshead in 2008. The list of famous footballing names goes on and on: Chris Waddle, Frank Clark, Norman Hunter, Steve Stone and, of course, Paul 'Gazza' Gascoigne; however, we're going to look at a player who may be a little less well known when compared to the household names above, despite being capped sixty-five times for his country and captaining them at the 1974 World Cup in West Germany.

Peter Wilson

Peter 'Big Willie' Wilson was born in Felling on 15 September 1947 and began his footballing career at Middlesbrough. Between the years of 1966 and 1968 he appeared only once for the first team in a Division Two league game home to Charlton Athletic in February 1968. After a brief spell with his hometown club, Gateshead FC, in which he made only two appearances, he emigrated to Australia in January 1969 aged only twenty. He signed for South Coast United and, having failed to make his big break in English football, he was about to embark on a career in Australia that would see him become a national hero thousands of miles away from his country of birth.

Wilson signed for South Coast United and played his first game on 19 January 1969, instantly making an impact as 'Big Willie' and reinventing himself as a tough but fair defender with wild hair and a handlebar moustache. He had been a right-back but an injury to another defender saw him moved to sweeper and he looked immediately at home. In his first season he helped South Coast, who had been languishing near the bottom of the league, to win the Championship of the New South Wales League State. In 1970 his impressive form saw him called up for the Australian international side, and in 1971, after only a handful of caps, he was appointed captain of the national side.

In 1974 he led his adopted homeland to qualification in their first ever World Cup. Drawn in the 'group of death', Wilson captained his side to a 2-0 defeat to East Germany,

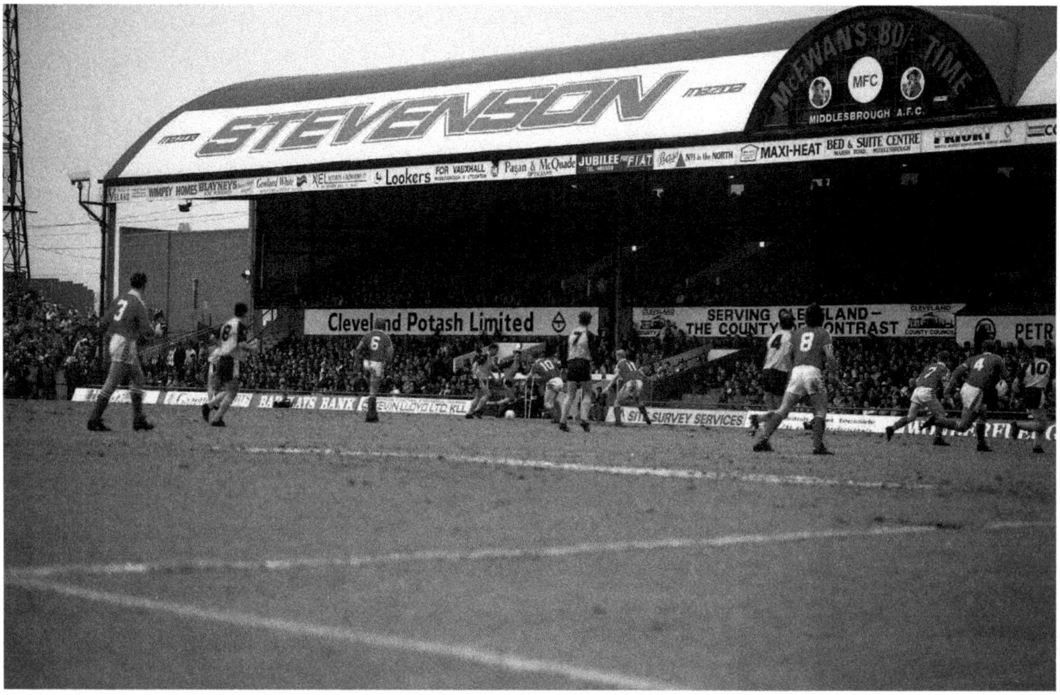

Ayresome Park, erstwhile Stadium of Middlesbrough FC – where Peter Wilson began his footballing career.

a 3-0 loss to hosts – and eventual winners – West Germany, and then a hard fought goalless draw with Chile. Despite elimination from the tournament Wilson impressed on the world stage, and the East Germany game in particular has been described as the finest ninety minutes of his career.

After the defeat to West Germany, Gerd Muller said of Wilson, 'He is the roughest man I've played against. He didn't seem to care whether he kicked the ball, a leg, or a head.'

After elimination from the tournament, Wilson's excellent displays led to some European newspapers described him as being one of the best talents in world football, calling him the Australian Beckenbauer. His fantastic form saw offers from several top English clubs give him a chance to return home, there were also offers on the table from some of Germany's top sides; however he decided to stay in Australia, a country he now considered his home.

Peter went on to play for the Australian national team for a decade, officially winning sixty-four caps and captaining the side sixty times – a record that still stands to this day.

Following his retirement in 1982 he has remained in Australia and lived a quiet life, staying out of the public eye. He was the only player not to turn up to a 1974 World Cup reunion in 1997. Despite this he remains a national hero and even had a street named after him in Sydney, but he did not attend the inauguration of the 'Peter Wilson Street' when it was unveiled in 2000.

William Shield

Let's now take a look at the life and career of a musician born in Swalwell, who may have written and composed an incredibly famous tune, most usually credited to Scottish poet Robbie Burns.

William Shield was born on 5 March 1748. As a child, at the age of six, his dad taught him to play the violin. However the death of his mother, and then his father, saw the now orphaned William apprenticed to a shipbuilder in South Shields. He soon returned to his love of music, though, studying under Charles Avison, the organist at St John's Church in Newcastle.

St John's Church in Sunderland was consecrated in 1769 and Shield composed the anthem. He moved to Scarborough and led an orchestra there. The reputation he had built saw him move once again to London, where Italian composer Felice Giardini appointed him to play the violin at Covent Garden. In 1773 he became principal violinist. At Covent Garden he was also working as a composer and met Joseph Haydn, an Austrian composer who was a friend and mentor of Mozart and teacher of Beethoven.

In 1817 he was given the post of Master of the King's Musick, serving George III and later George IV, with compositions and direction of the court orchestra as and when required.

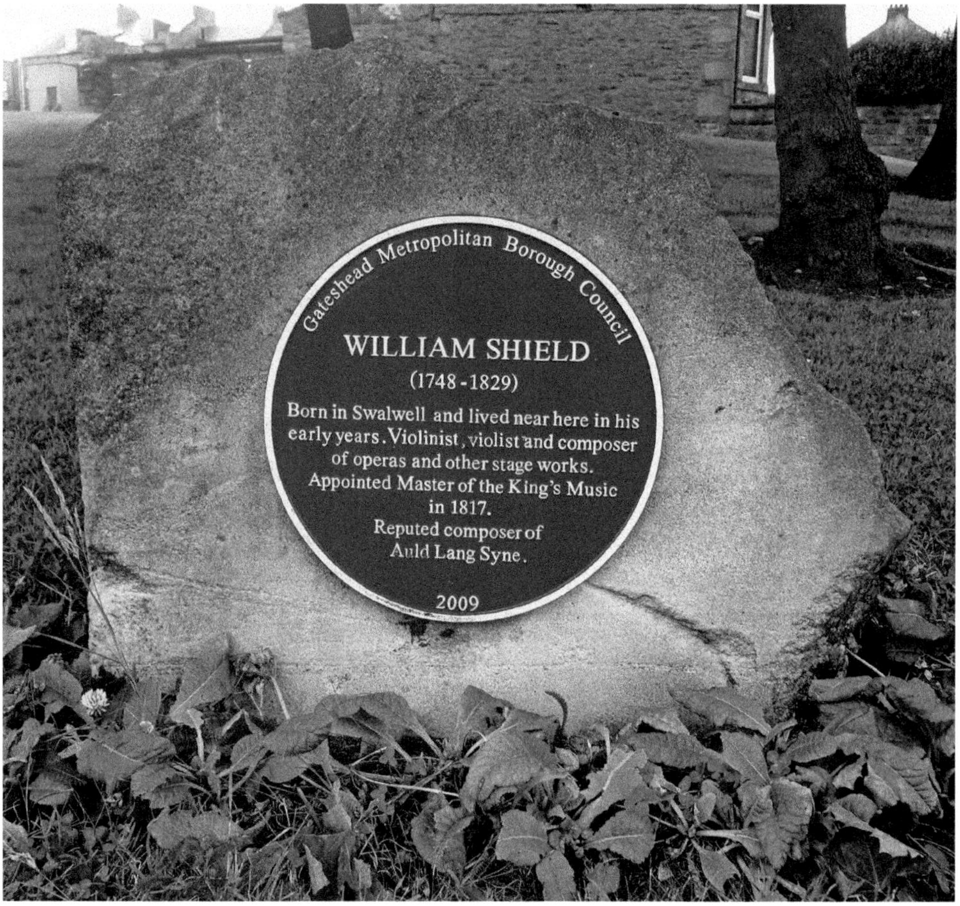

William Shield's blue plaque on Hood Street, Swalwell.

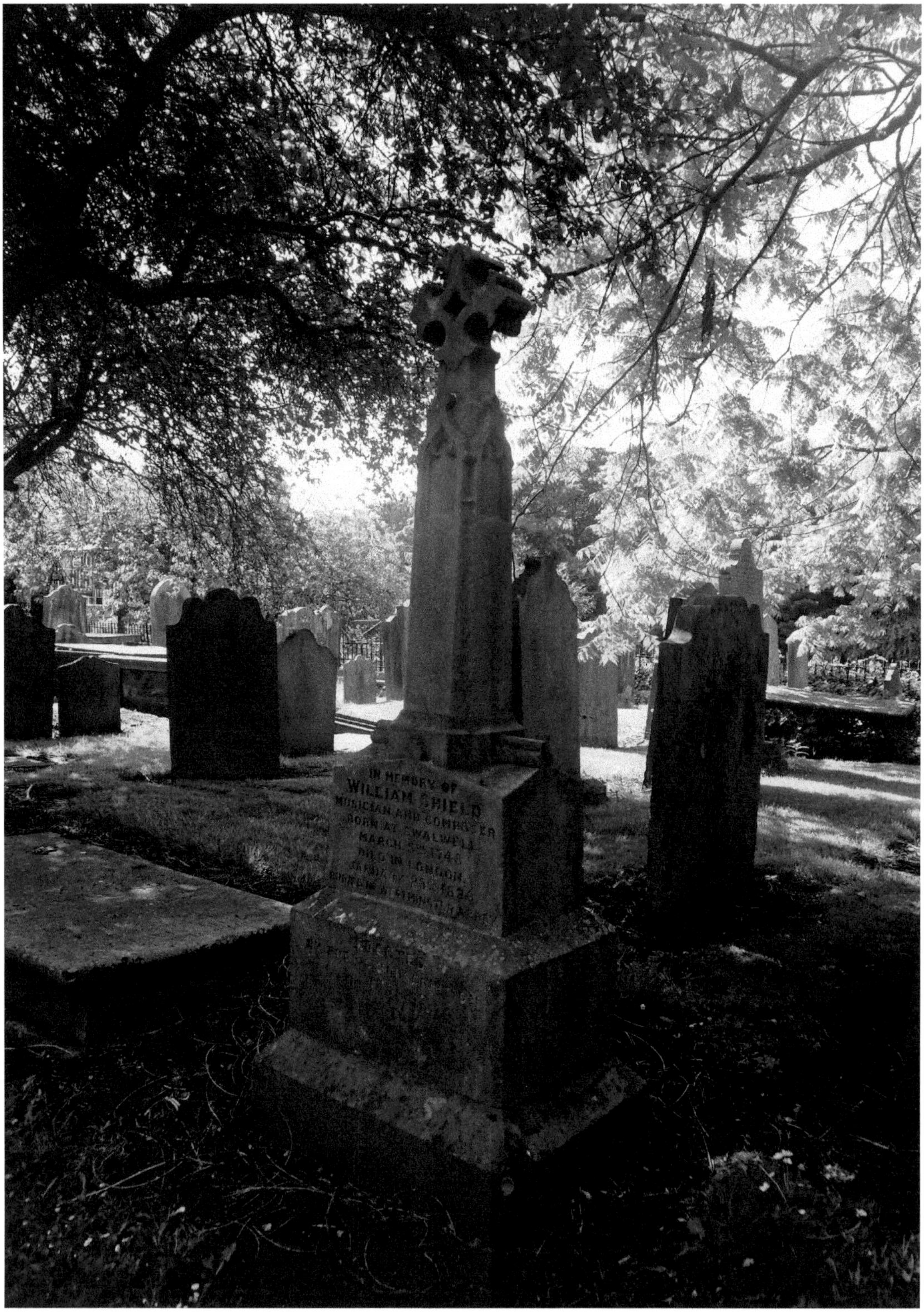

William Shield memorial cross at Whickham Church.

He composed over thirty operas, his first being the *Flitch of Bacon* in 1778. He composed a large number of other stage works. His best known work is his English light opera Rosina from 1781.

On Sunday 25th January 1829 William Shield passed away at his home in London. He was buried at Westminster Abbey at the request of George IV, as Shield was a favourite of the king. Shield's favourite Stainer viola was in his will to go to the king. Unusually, no kind of marker was placed to show where he had been laid to rest in the south cloisters, although we do know he was buried in the same grave as Johann Peter Salomon, a German musician who Shield had played violin with at Covent Garden. At the centenary of his death a search was made for Shield's grave, and a marble tablet was put in place where it was believed he had been laid to rest.

William Shield may be best known these days for the controversy surrounding claims made long after his passing that he wrote the tune of 'Auld Lang Syne', the song famously sung every New Year and credited to Robbie Burns. This had been debated regularly throughout the nineteenth and twentieth centuries, and the theory relates to a melody at the end of the *Rosina* overture, which bears a striking resemblance to the tune of 'Auld Land Syne'. This was thrust back into the public spotlight in 1998 when John Treherne, Head of Gateshead Schools Music Service, discovered an original edition of the opera in Gateshead's Central Library. He said, at the time, when seeking out work for the town's youth orchestra, 'I thought it was appropriate to look at the work of a Gateshead-born composer. I picked out Rosina by Shield. I started to copy out the score and hummed the tune as I was writing it down. I was coming to the end when I realised the tune floating through my head was Auld Lang Syne.' This led to headlines in national newspapers such as 'England Lays Claim to Auld Lang Syne', which sparked a bit of a backlash from those north of the border.

The truth is that it's most likely that Shield borrowed the tune from an existing folk tune, likely lost to time. Shield, as many composers of his day, would often reuse folk tunes, most commonly from his native north-east and Northumberland in particular. Interestingly, Burns actually never claimed to have written the song in the first place. 'I took it down from an old man's singing,' he wrote in 1793, in a note accompanying the lyrics to 'Auld Lang Syne'. He sent it to James Johnson, the editor of the *Scots Musical Museum*, adding that it was 'an olden song that had never been written down'.

Arthur Holmes

Moving on from a famous musician hailing from Gateshead, we'll now look at a true 'rock' star, a geologist who first dated our planet Earth.

Arthur Holmes was born along the Tyne at Hebburn on 14 January 1890 but grew up in Low Fell, attending the Gateshead Higher Grade School, which would later be known as Gateshead Grammar School. At the age of seventeen he enrolled onto a course to study Physics at the Royal College of Science, however the following year he realised where his true passion lay, and switched to geology.

Upon his graduation in 1910 he entered into the failed venture of prospecting for minerals in Mozambique. Over the six months that he was there he found nothing, and contracted malaria. He was so ill that notice of his death was sent home to his parents. Thankfully he made a surprise recovery and headed back to England. Between the years of 1912 and 1920 he became a demonstrator at Imperial College. During his time in Mozambique he achieved little financially but amassed a wealth of knowledge, particularly with regards to geochronology, such as the ability to be able to measure the radioactive decay of uranium found within rocks to accurately date them. He would put this to good use in writing a number of pioneering works, of which his most famous, *The Age of the Earth*, was published in 1913, where he estimated the age of the earth as at least 1.6 billion years old. This publication would lead to Holmes being the leading figure in this field throughout the rest of his career, being nicknamed the Father of Modern Geochronology.

In 1920, after obtaining a Doctorate of Science, he left for Burma, joining an oil company as chief geologist. This was another failed venture overseas, however, and he returned home three years later without a penny to his name.

He joined Durham University in the newly created role of Reader in Geology, and it was here where he had his most productive years. He re-founded the department and, as

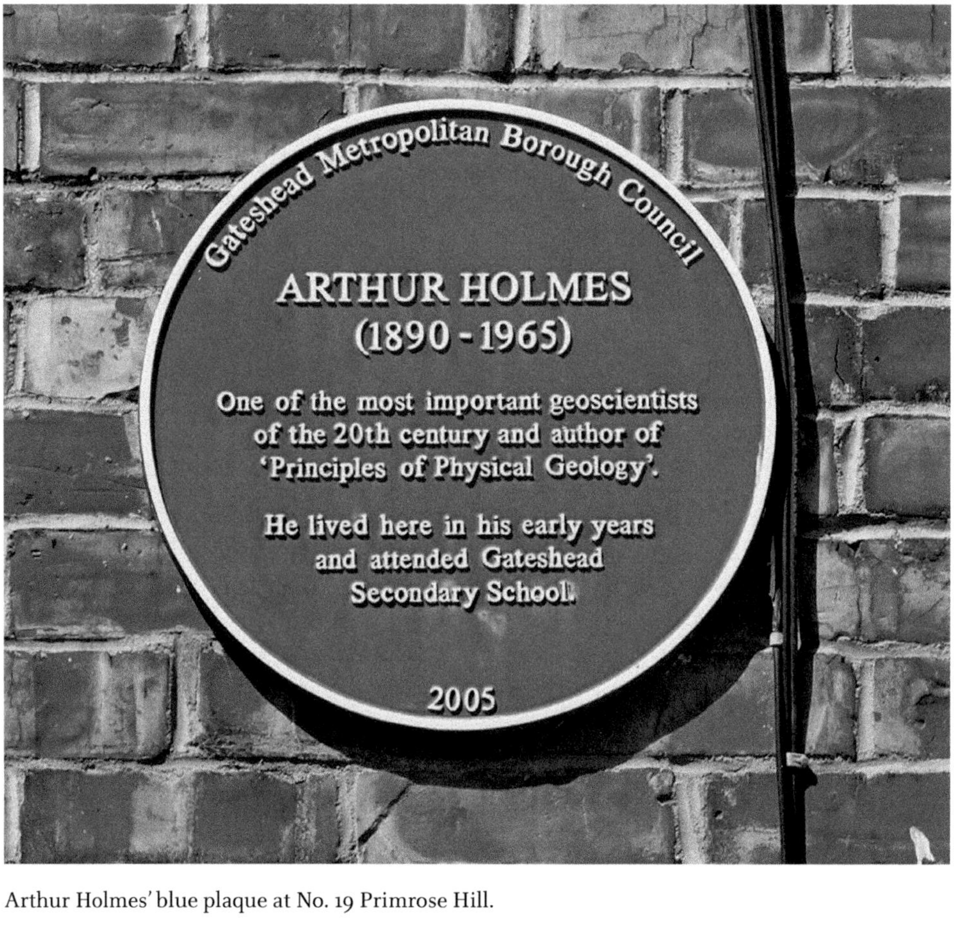

Arthur Holmes' blue plaque at No. 19 Primrose Hill.

advancements continued to be made in the field of geochronology, he would revise his timescale of Earth as it soon became clear that it was considerably older than his original estimation. By the time his final timescale was published, he dated Earth at 4,550 million years old. This is still accepted as its age.

In 1942 he became a Fellow of the Royal Society, an award and fellowship granted by the Royal Society of London to individuals the society judges to have made a 'substantial contribution to the improvement of natural knowledge, including mathematics, engineering science and medical science'. The following year he moved to the University of Edinburgh and was appointed to the post of Chair of Geology.

By the time he retired in 1956 he had received many more international honours, including the Penrose Medal and Wollaston Medal, whose previous winners included Charles Darwin. Arthur Holmes died on 20 September 1965 in Putney, London, aged seventy-five.

He has left a lasting legacy, Durham University's Department of Earth Sciences' Isotope Geology Laboratory is named after him, as is the student's Geology Society. There is even a crater on Mars named in his honour. His writing is considered essential reading in the field, and his methods are still used to this very day.

Colin Armstrong

Next, we'll move on to Colin Armstrong, who was born in Rowlands Gill in 1961 and is better known by his pen name and pseudonym, Chris Ryan. He was an SAS war hero, and an author and television personality.

He went to Hookergate School in High Spen and then, from the age of sixteen, the army became his life, becoming a boy soldier and then later joining the Special Air Service (SAS) in 1984. During his ten years in the SAS he was involved in operations across the world, as well as being sniper team commander of an anti-terrorist unit.

In January 1991, during the Gulf War, Ryan was a member of an eight-man SAS patrol with call sign Bravo Two Zero. They were sent behind enemy lines to a main supply route between Baghdad and north-west Iraq to gather intelligence, find a good position and set up an observation post. They were compromised, however, and forced to head north to Syria on foot. Three of his colleagues were killed and four were captured. Ryan was the only one to escape.

He made SAS history with the longest escape and evasion by an SAS trooper or any other soldier, covering 180 miles to get to the Syrian border. During this escape he lost a potentially fatal amount of weight, and survived by drinking water contaminated with nuclear waste. He suffered from post-traumatic stress disorder after this and didn't return to operational duty. He spent his remaining three years in the SAS selecting and training potential recruits, before being honourably discharged in 1994.

On 29 June 1991 he was awarded the Military Medal 'in recognition of gallant and distinguished services in the Gulf in 1991'.

Since leaving the SAS Ryan has gone on to find fame writing several bestselling books, some of which have been adapted for television. He's also acted and presented in a number of popular television shows including *Ultimate Force*, which he co-created, *Hunting Chris Ryan*, and *How Not to Die*.

DID YOU KNOW?
Chris Ryan has written a romantic novel, *The Fisherman's Daughter*, under the pseudonym Molly Jackson.

Sarah Emily Davies

After looking at a war hero from Gateshead, let's now look at another hero in a very different field. Sarah Emily Davies was born in Southampton on 22 April 1830, the daughter of John Davies and Mary Hopkinson; however, Emily, as she was known, grew up in Gateshead, where her father was rector and her mother was a teacher.

Emily was homeschooled – typical for girls of the time – whereas her three brothers were sent away to boarding school. Along with her sister Jane, her education focused mainly on how to perform household duties. She also helped to nurse two of her siblings, Jane and Henry, through tuberculosis.

Emily was very close to her older brother John Llewelyn, and his success at Cambridge University made her realise how she had been denied an equal opportunity to an academic education simply because she was female.

In her twenties Emily considered a career in medicine, and would later become close friends with Elizabeth Garrett, who herself had ambitions to become a doctor and would go on to become the first woman in Britain to qualify as a surgeon and physician. However Emily's poor education would ultimately make this an impossible career option. Frustration at her unfair start in life, due to her gender, led her to make the decision to join other like-minded females and dedicate her life to helping other young woman to obtain the opportunities she had been denied.

In 1862, after her father passed away, she moved to London with her mother. She edited the *English Woman's Journal* and became friends with women's rights advocates Barbara Bodichon, Elizabeth Garrett and her younger sister Millicent Fawcett.

Emily's first campaign was to persuade the authorities to allow girls to be admitted to secondary school examinations, and women to have equal rights to men regarding degrees and teaching qualifications. In 1864, Emily had her first success when the Schools Enquiry Commission agreed to look into gender inequalities in education.

In 1865 Emily became a founder member of a women's discussion group, the Kensington Society, along with Dorothea Beale, Elizabeth Garrett, Barbara Bodichon and Francis Mary Buss. The following year the group formed the London Suffrage Committee and began organising a petition asking Parliament to grant women the vote. She also became involved in the suffrage movement, which centred on achieving the woman's right to vote. In 1866 she was involved in John Stuart Mill's 1866 petition to the British Parliament, which was the first to ask for women's suffrage. That same year she also wrote the book *The Higher Education of Women.*

In 1869, she was part of a group that funded and opened Girton College – the first college for women. In 1873 the college moved to the outskirts of Cambridge, though it wasn't until April 1948 that female students at Girton would be admitted full membership

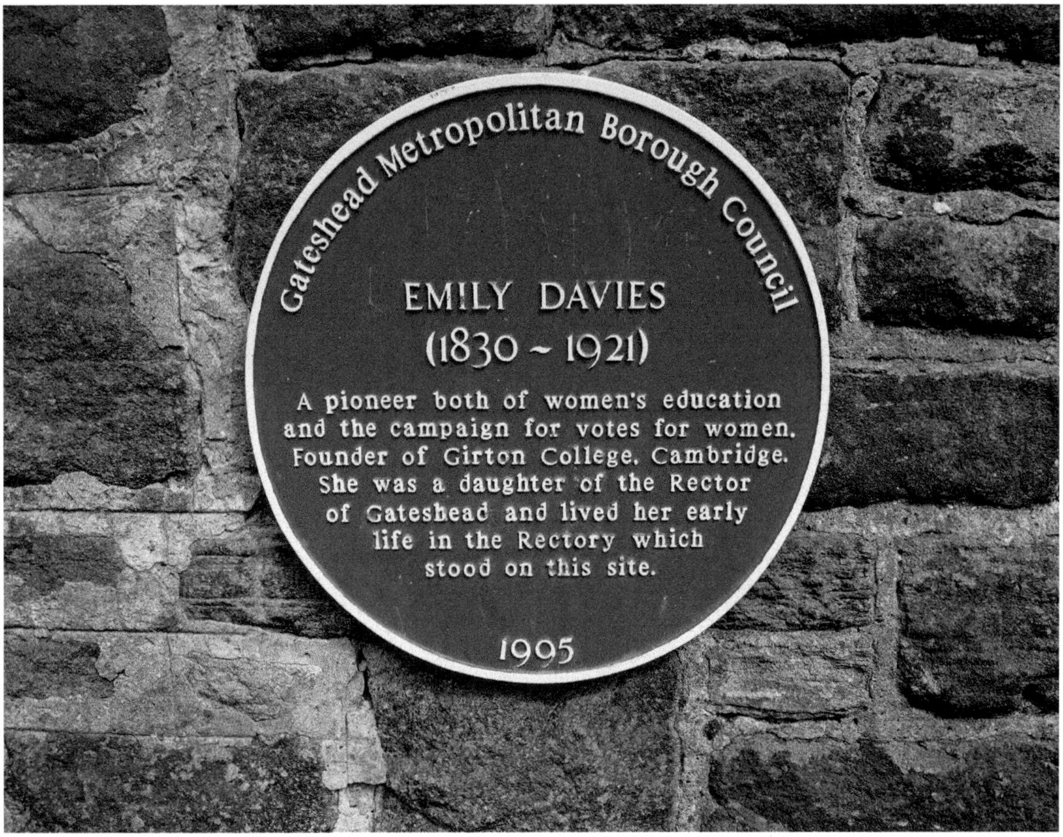

Emily Davies' blue plaque where Rectory Road meets Bensham Road.

of the University of Cambridge. Emily served as mistress of the college from 1873–75, and then would serve as secretary until 1904.

In 1889 Emily returned to the struggle for the vote when she joined the committee of the London National Society for Women's Suffrage. In 1901 she was awarded an honorary Doctor of Laws (DLL) from the University of Glasgow. In 1919 Davies was one of the very few early members of the first Women's Suffrage Society still left alive to record their vote in a parliamentary election.

Emily Davies died on 13 July 1921. Today a blue plaque marks the site in Gateshead where the rectory in which she grew up once stood. In north-west Cambridge 'Davies' was approved in 2016 for use as a future street name for a new development.

Henry Clasper

Henry 'Harry' Clasper was born in Dunston on 5 July 1812 and would become an internally recognised sporting superstar, one of – if not the – most famous sportsmen in Great Britain at the time.

Clasper was one of a family of fifteen and was born into a humble life. The family moved to Jarrow when he was young and, at the age of fifteen, he began to work at Jarrow

Pit. Clasper soon decided that mining wasn't for him and he became ship's carpenter's apprentice in Brown's Boatyard.

In 1836 he was married to Susannah Hawks – his cousin. He couldn't read or write so signed the wedding certificate with a cross, whereas his new bride signed her name.

Clasper, having gained invaluable experience in boat building from his former employment, formed a racing crew with his brother William, John Thompson, Robert Dinning, and another brother, Robert, as cox in a boat was named the *Swalwell*. At the time rowers were the first modern sporting superstars. The riverside was crowded by up to 100,000 people for races, as entry cost nothing. Clasper's team got off to a great start, winning races, gaining a reputation locally, and became known as the Derwenthaugh crew.

Clasper took over the tenancy of the Skiff Inn on the Gateshead side of the Tyne, and, in addition to being the landlord, he built himself boats on the same site. He built two skiffs for himself: *The Hawk* in 1840 and *The Young Hawk* in 1841. With the latter, he won the Durham Regatta Single Sculls race in 1842.

The Derwenthaugh crew was dominating the rowing scene on the Tyne and the logical progression was to challenge a crew from the River Thames. This was done and the race was held on the Tyne on 16 July 1842. The race was rowed over a 5-mile course from the Tyne for a stake of £150 a side. The Thames crew gained an easy victory. Clasper's crew's boat, *St Agnes*, although much narrower than the Thames boat, was far heavier.

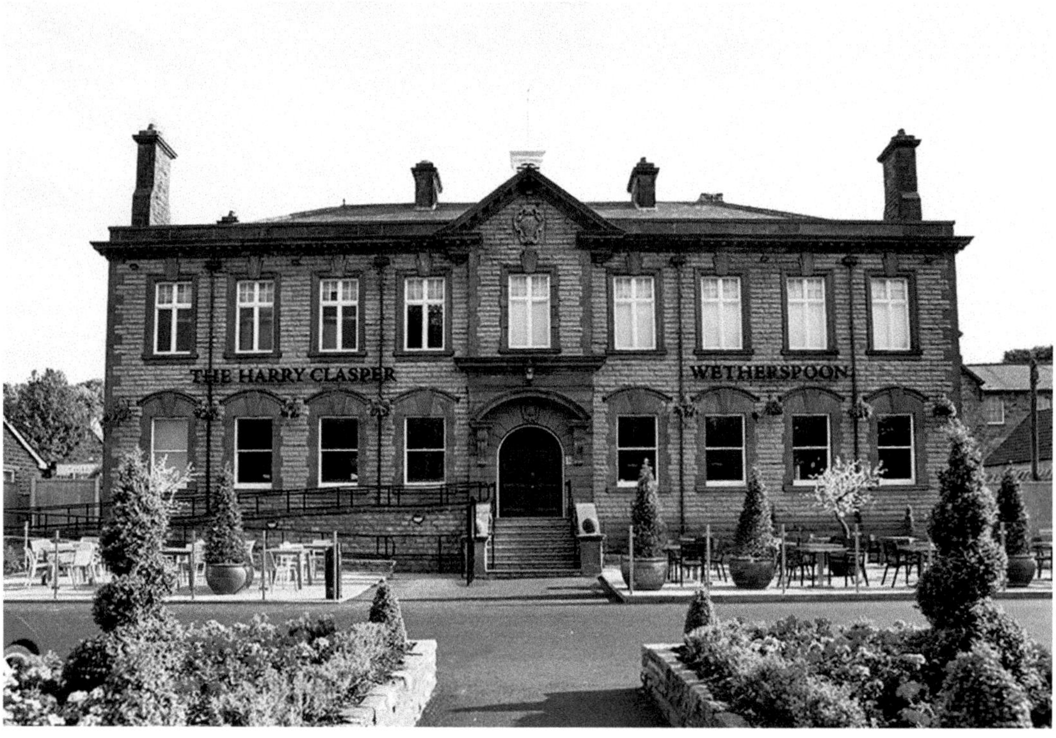

The Harry Clasper Wetherspoons pub in Whickham.

Despite the humiliating defeat, Harry had an overriding determination to win. He took a valuable lesson from the race and set about designing a far lighter boat for his crew; his subsequent boats would see him incorporate a number of revolutionary designs that are still used this very day.

His next boat, *The Five Brothers*, was far lighter, and when it made an appearance at the Thames Regatta in 1844 the Derwenthaugh crew won a prize of £50, narrowly missing winning the £100 top prize of the Champion Fours. Clasper and his crew were back for the Thames Regatta the following year. This time they took another four-oared boat, *The Lord Ravensworth*. This latest boat was a further improvement on *The Five Brothers*. The crew were all Claspers: Harry and his brothers William and Robert, their uncle Ned as the fourth oarsman, and brother Richard as cox. The Derwenthaugh crew won the Champion Fours, beating two other crews including the 'unbeatable' London rowers. They were awarded the title of four-oared world champions. The victory caused a national sensation and the crew were given a hero's welcome on returning to Newcastle.

Over the next fifteen years, Clasper, with a variety of other crewmembers, including his eldest son John Hawks Clasper, won the Champion Fours at the Thames Regatta a further six times. He retired from rowing in 1867, having raced around 130 times in his career and

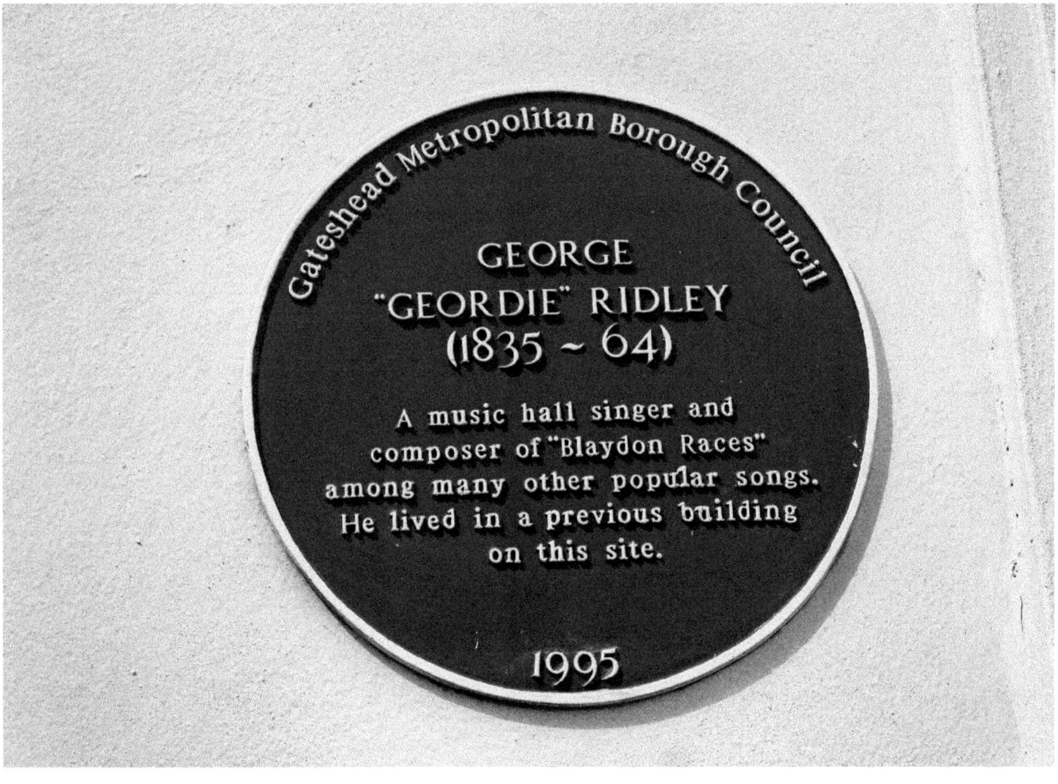

George 'Geordie' Ridley blue plaque at the William IV pub, High Street. The building was once his home.

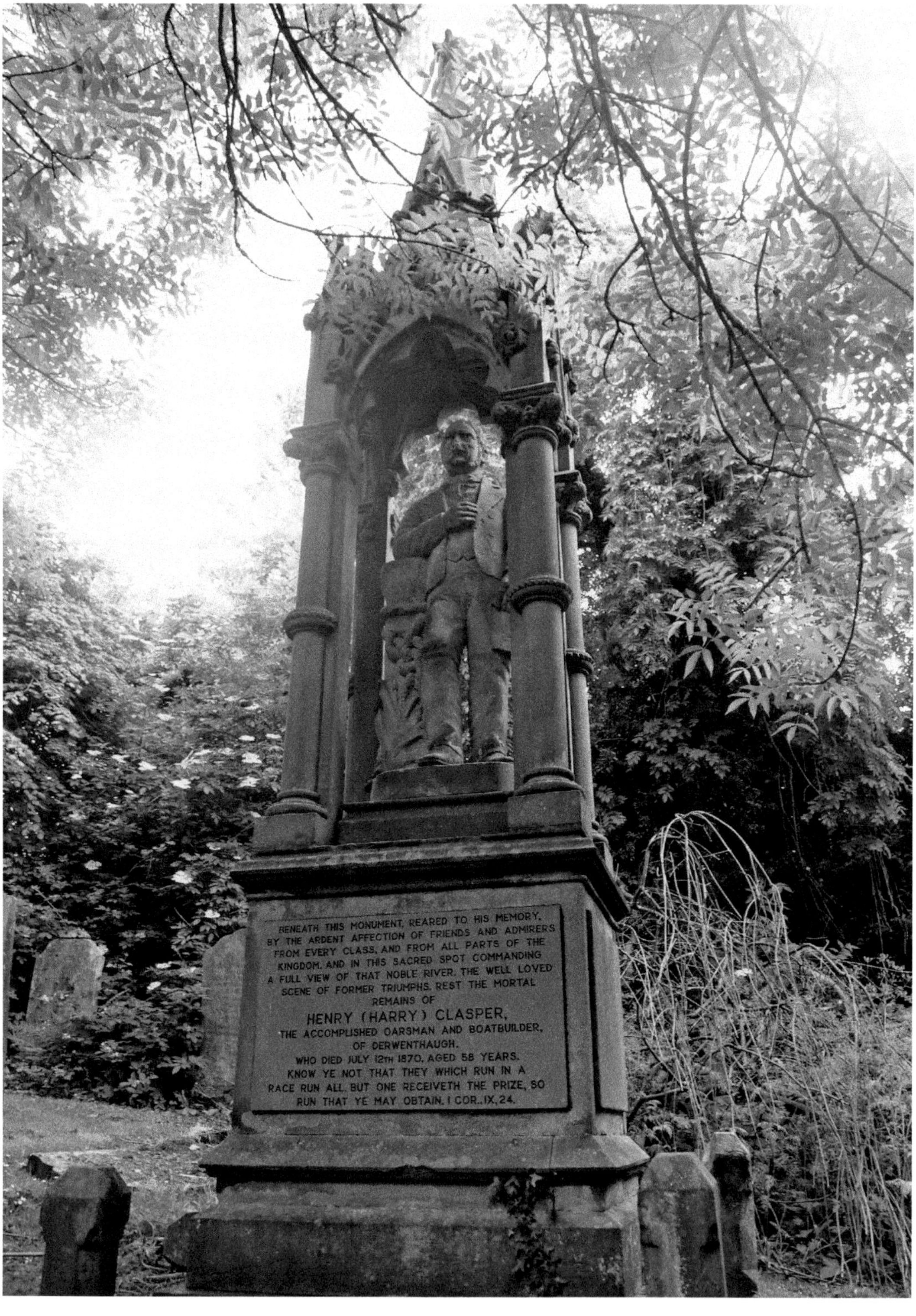

Harry Clasper grave and memorial at Whickham Church.

become a megastar. In 1868, a testimonial evening was held for him at Balmbra's Music Hall in Newcastle. A never-before heard tune called the 'Blaydon Races', written especially for the occasion, was premiered.

DID YOU KNOW?

George 'Geordie' Ridley wrote the Blaydon Races for Harry Clapser's testimonial evening, and coincidentally also once worked at one of Clasper's former employers when he was employed as a waggon-rider at Hawks, Crawshay and Sons for three years.

Clasper became a rowing coach and coached Robert Chambers from Walker, who became Tyne, Thames and England world sculling champion.

Clasper died on 12 July 1870 aged fifty-eight. His funeral saw his coffin transported from the Tunnel Inn in Ouseburn, which he had been running at the time of his death, to St Mary's Church in Whickham. Part of the journey saw the coffin taken by boat along the River Tyne, travelling over part of the course that he knew so well in life. Over 130,000 people turned out to pay their respects.

3. Crime and Punishment

The first ever recorded murders in Gateshead happened in 1080 in a series of horrific, brutal incidents, which left a bloody stain on the history of the town.

William Walcher was from Lotharingia, which comprised of modern-day Netherlands, Belgium, Luxemberg, France and parts of Germany. Following the Norman Conquest he was appointed to the role of Bishop of Durham in *c.* 1071 by William I, better known as William the Conqueror. In 1076, he bought the earldom of Northumberland after the beheading of his friend Waltheof, the last Saxon Earl of Northumbria. This execution, for treason, took place on 31 May 1076 on the orders of William I. He was the only major noble executed by the Norman king.

DID YOU KNOW?

On 1 October 1968, Gateshead Police Force, which consisted of 214 members of staff, were merged with Durham County Police.

After Waltheof's death, Ligulf of Lumley was one of the last remaining noblemen in the north with connections to Bamburgh, and he was married to Ealdgyth, the daughter of Earl Ealdred of Bernicia. He became one of Walcher's main advisors; however he didn't see eye to eye with Walcher's chaplain Leobwin and his kinsman Gilbert, who themselves, alongside a number of Walcher's ministers, were guilty of abusing their power to commit a number of wrongdoings to the Northumbrian people.

In 1079 the Scottish invaded Northumbria, led by Malcolm III. Walcher was unable – or unwilling – to prevent the attack, and the Scots raped and pillaged their way across Northumbria unopposed. When they eventually headed back over the border three weeks later they took all the valuables they could carry and a great number of Northumbrians to be used as slaves.

Ligulf was very critical of Walcher's inability to handle the situation and believed he had let his people down. Leobwin and Gilbert took offence to this and in April 1080 (though some accounts say early May) they led an attack on Ligulf's house in the middle of the night and killed almost all of the household, including Ligulf himself. The attack was aided by Walcher's own knights, but it is not clear as to whether Walcher himself had knowledge of the plot. Ligulf's wife, Ealgyth, was spared in the attack and afterwards Walcher offered her a gift of land to settle the feud.

Despite Walcher's insistence of not being involved in the murder, no effort made to bring the murderers to justice. Ligulf was hugely popular with the Northumbrians due to his nationality, rank, and virtues, and his murder caused great anger across Northumbria. Rebellion seemed almost certain, so Walcher agreed to meet the enraged people – led by Eadulf Rus, the leader of the kinsman – at Gateshead. The choice of Gateshead as a meeting place shows the importance of the location in eleventh-century Northumbria.

DID YOU KNOW?

In 1627, Gateshead parish was fined a sum of 6*s* 8*d* by the justices of the peace because the town did not possess a ducking stool. The ducking stool was the traditional punishment for disorderly wives. This omission was rectified the following year. It was used so often that it had to be replaced in 1660.

Walcher took over 100 followers to the meeting for his safety, but they were still outnumbered by the Northumbrians. Walcher was presented with a list of his crimes against the local people, which he denied, and so the enraged Northumbrians attacked the Norman party. Walcher retreated into a small church (near the site of the current St Mary's Church) with his surviving followers. The crowd surrounded the church and Walcher sent a reluctant Gilbert out to attempt to calm the baying mob. He didn't get chance; as soon as he appeared he was slaughtered.

When the bishop didn't come out of the church, the crowd set fire to the building. As the flames ripped through the structure, those taking refuge were forced into the open. Walcher was set upon straight away and brutally murdered. Leobwin was also killed, along with many of the bishop's followers. The monks at Jarrow later found Walcher's body and took it back to their monastery; it was later moved to Durham for a private burial.

Following the killing of the bishop, the rebels attacked Walcher's castle at Durham and besieged it for four days. William I sent his half-brother, Odo of Bayeux, to lead an army to harry the Northumbrian countryside. The power of the Anglo-Saxon nobility in Northumbria was lost and many of the native nobility were driven into hiding.

On 20 January 1836 John Usher was appointed as Gateshead's first ever police constable, and the following week he was promoted to superintendent. By the end of April six constables were employed to work alongside Usher. In these early days, the job mainly involved chasing thieves and patrolling the old turnpike road. By the end of the decade Gateshead's police force had two lock-ups for prisoners, one of which was in the town hall and the other on the Gateshead site of the Tyne Bridge. In 1845 the River Tyne Police started patrolling the river in rowing boats; they'd later get their own purpose-built police station at the Gateshead side of the Swing Bridge, which opened in 1910.

During the 1840s Gateshead police were permitted to carry sticks, but in 1853 this was forbidden and they were told to 'control their tempers'.

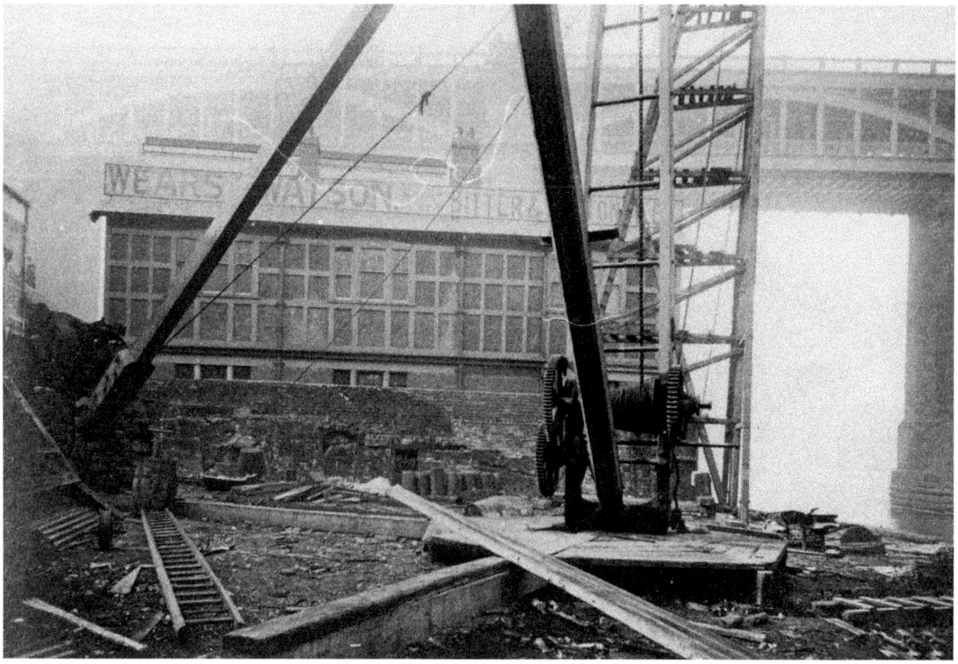

Gateshead River Police Station being constructed in 1910. (Photo courtesy of Gateshead Libraries)

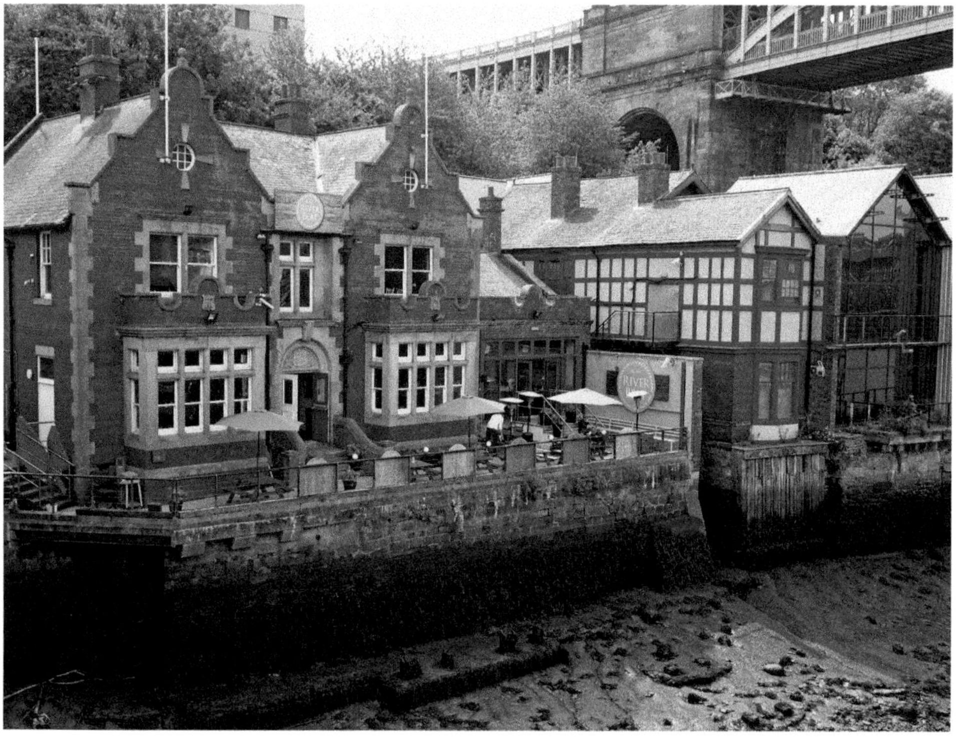

The former River Police Station in 2017, now the River Beat restaurant.

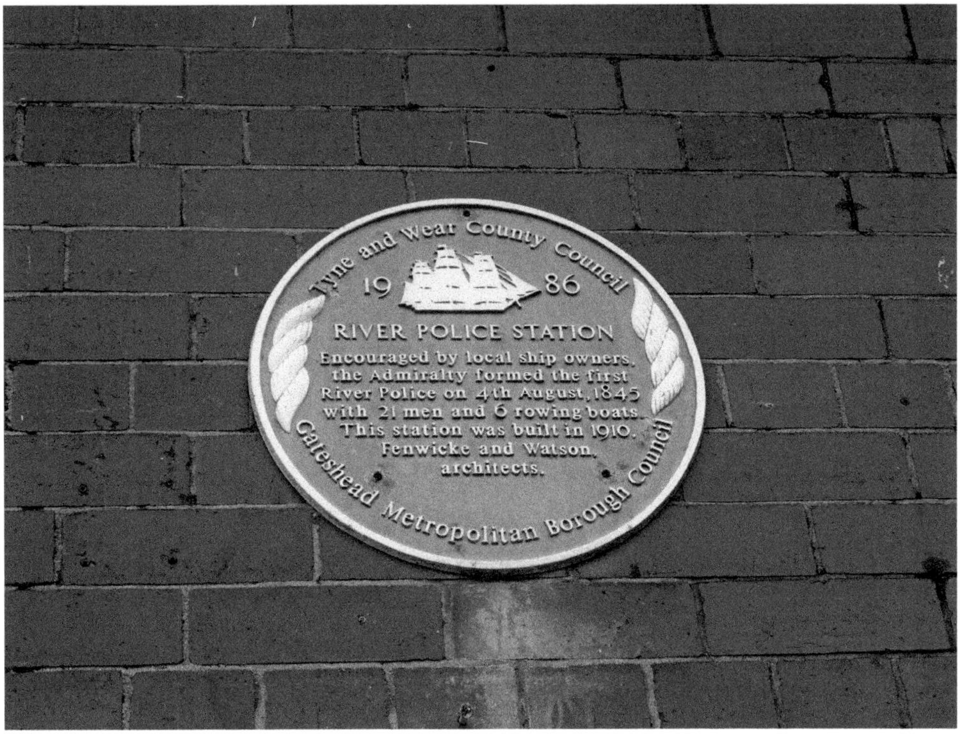

The River Police Station blue plaque.

In early 1889 one of Usher's colleagues, John Graham, was brutally murdered in Wrekenton by Edward Wilkinson; the chillingly nicknamed 'Flying Butcher' (due to his profession as a casual butcher). Graham was twenty-nine years old, married with four children, and had only become a policeman the previous year. Graham had testified the previous month against Wilkinson on a charge of disorder, which saw him fined 2*s* 6*d*.

The 'disorder' had occurred on 16 January 1889; Wilkinson had been in the process of evicting his wife from their small home when Graham was called to the scene and had a word with Wilkinson. He didn't appreciate this advice and flew into a rage, grabbing a poker and threatening the policeman. His threat was repeated following the fine, when he promised to 'fettle' PC Graham. True to his word, when Wilkinson saw PC Graham on his beat passing outside his house in broad daylight, he grabbed a knife. Wilkinson's wife begged him to stop, but he battered her to the ground. The streets were busy with people going about their lives. Wilkinson crept behind the policeman, who was unaware of Wilkinson's presence. Grabbing the policeman from behind, he swung him around and plunged the knife deeply into the right side of the Graham's chest. Wilkinson's neighbours looked on in horror. PC Graham tried to escape but collapsed on the ground, holding his bleeding chest. Wilkinson grabbed the truncheon from his belt and rained down powerful blows on the policeman's head.

Search parties were sent out to bring the Flying Butcher to justice and he was captured at the Railway Tavern in South Hylton, Sunderland, with the murder weapon secured to his leg by a garter. When he was asked about the crime he said, 'I know all about that.' Justice was swift: on 26 February Edward Wilkinson was found guilty of murder at Durham Assizes, where he interrupted the sentencing judge with a cry of: 'Oh let's have it! It's no use bothering'. He was sentenced to hang, but managed to escape the gallows on the grounds of insanity.

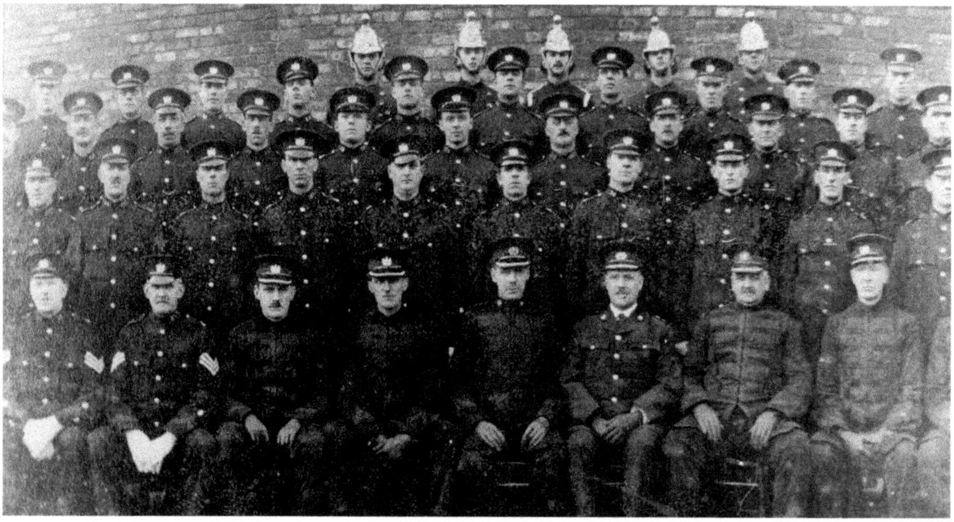

The Gateshead Borough police force in 1925. (Photo courtesy of Gateshead Libraries)

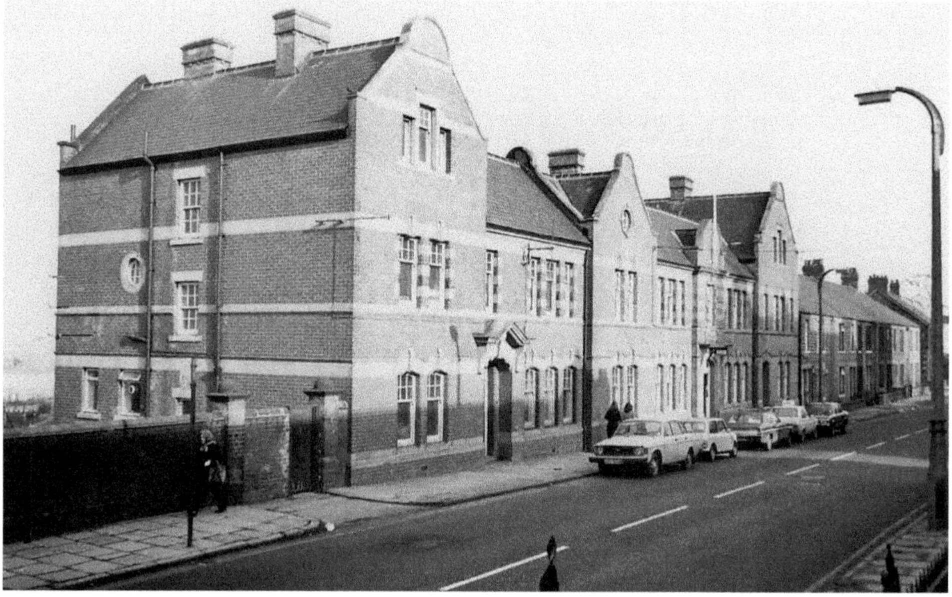

Felling Police Station built around 1906 and located on Sunderland Road. The station closed in October 1999. (Photo courtesy of Gateshead Libraries)

Someone who wasn't quite as fortunate was highwayman Robert Hazlett, who, in 1770, was convicted of committing two acts of highway robbery in the same night. In the first instance he robbed a lady named Miss Margaret Benson, who had been travelling from Durham to Newcastle. He put his pistol to her head and demanded her watch and purse. Afterwards Hazlett continued along the turnpike and encountered a postman, who, despite having been forewarned by Miss Benson, was 'lured into a trap' and robbed. He attempted a third, unsuccessful, robbery, and was later caught in South Shields.

Within one week of his arrest Hazlett was tried and convicted at the Newcastle Assizes. He was sentenced to hang, and became the first person to be gibbeted in the north-east following the Murder Act of 1752. His remains were hung in a gibbet cage as a warning to other potential would-be criminals near a pond at Beacon Lough on Gateshead Fell. That pond was named Hazlett's Pond in dubious honour of the highwayman, but has long since been drained and its precise location lost to time.

Mary Elizabeth Cassidy was born in Catchgate, Stanley, County Durham, on 11 June 1889. She married John Knowles from the quiet Gateshead suburb of Windy Nook on 9 September 1914, and lived there happily with him for over forty years until he passed away in 1955. Prior to John's death she had moved a lodger in by the name of John Russell and they had become lovers, unbeknown to her husband. Within two years he too had died. Inquests into the death of the two men determined both were due to natural causes. She inherited £42.

In June 1957, retired estate agent Oliver Leonard became Mary's second husband, but just twelve days into their marriage he had of heart failure, leaving her £100 in his will.

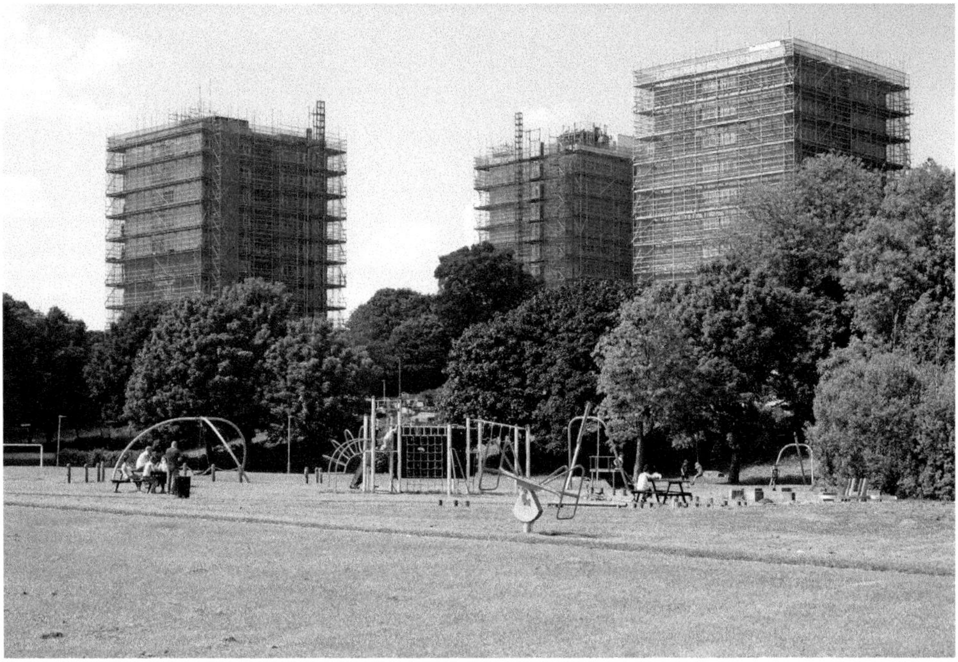

Beacon Lough, the approximate site of Robert Hazlett's gibbet.

Almost immediately she was wed for a third time – her second marriage that year – this time to Ernest Wilson. At the wedding one of the guests made a passing comment that the leftover sandwiches would go to waste, but Mary joked in front of the crowd: 'Don't worry, they'll keep for his funeral.'

Ernest fell ill almost immediately and died soon after of what the doctor called 'cardiac muscular failure'. This time she didn't even attend the funeral; however she inherited his bungalow, £100 in savings, and his life insurance payout.

Gossip quickly spread through Windy Nook of Mary's unfortunate luck with husbands and her cheery morbid humour towards it at her own wedding. When it was revealed that she had asked for a trade discount from the undertaker for providing him with so much business, she was brought to the attention of Gateshead police. The bodies of her last two husbands, Leonard and Wilson, were exhumed in 1958. Experts discovered abnormal amounts of toxins in their livers, which, along with traces of phosphorus, pointed to the use of beetle or rat poison. She was charged with the murders of the two men. Mary was tried and convicted in Leeds in 1958 and sentenced to death by hanging at Durham, though her age saw this reduced to life imprisonment.

The bodies of Knowles and Russell were later exhumed and the presence of phosphorus was once again determined as the cause of death, but there was no reason for a second trial. Mary died in 1963 in Holloway Prison at the age of seventy-four, and has gone down in history as the 'Merry Widow of Windy Nook'.

DID YOU KNOW?

Witches and witchcraft have been the cause of considerable superstition during the centuries, in particular the fifteenth–seventeenth centuries, with witchcraft becoming illegal in 1563 and punishable by death. In 1649–50 several women accused of witchcraft were arrested. They were tried at Durham and executed. The witch finder was awarded £2 10*d*.

I spoke to Andria Raistrick, who is the great-granddaughter of serial killer Mary Elizabeth Wilson. She is descended from Mary's marriage to John Knowles – her first husband, and first victim.

Andria told me she owns letters sent by Wilson to the prison governor 'asking to be sent to an old people's home instead of prison, so she could have peace and quiet'.

I asked Andria if she knew of any of the addresses Mary lived at and she told me 'there are two addresses on her marriage certificate to Ernest Wilson in 1957. Mary was living at 18 Collingwood Street, Hebburn, and Ernest was at 26 Rectory Road, Windy Nook.' I went to try and find these two houses, but neither is still standing. Andria also told me that 'the *News of the World* newspaper paid all of her legal fees so they could have exclusive rights to her story ... It's very strange having her as a great granny, it's horrible, but so interesting.'

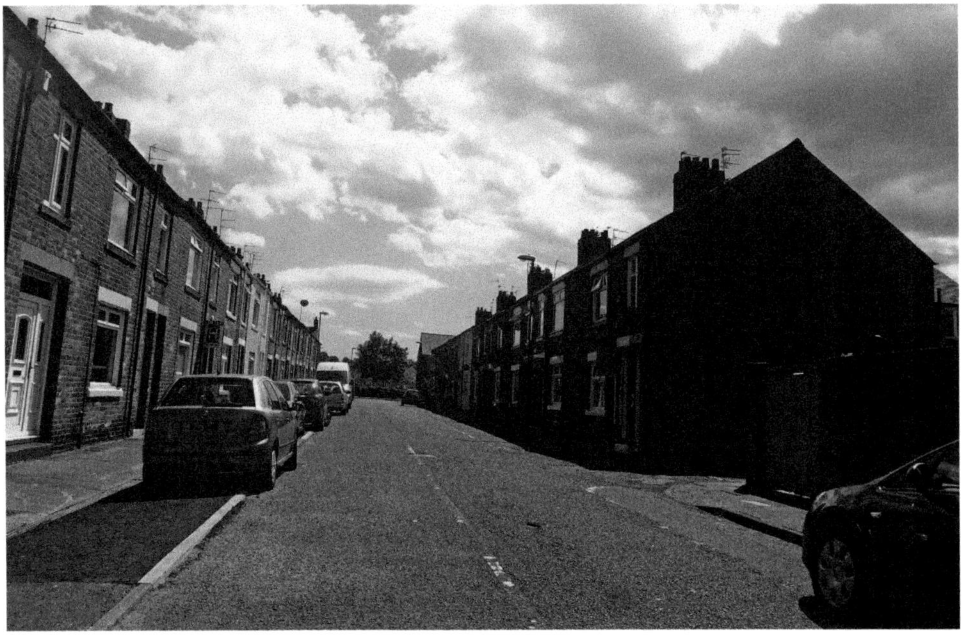

The remaining section of Collingwood Street, Hebburn. The Merry Widow of Windy Nook lived here in 1957.

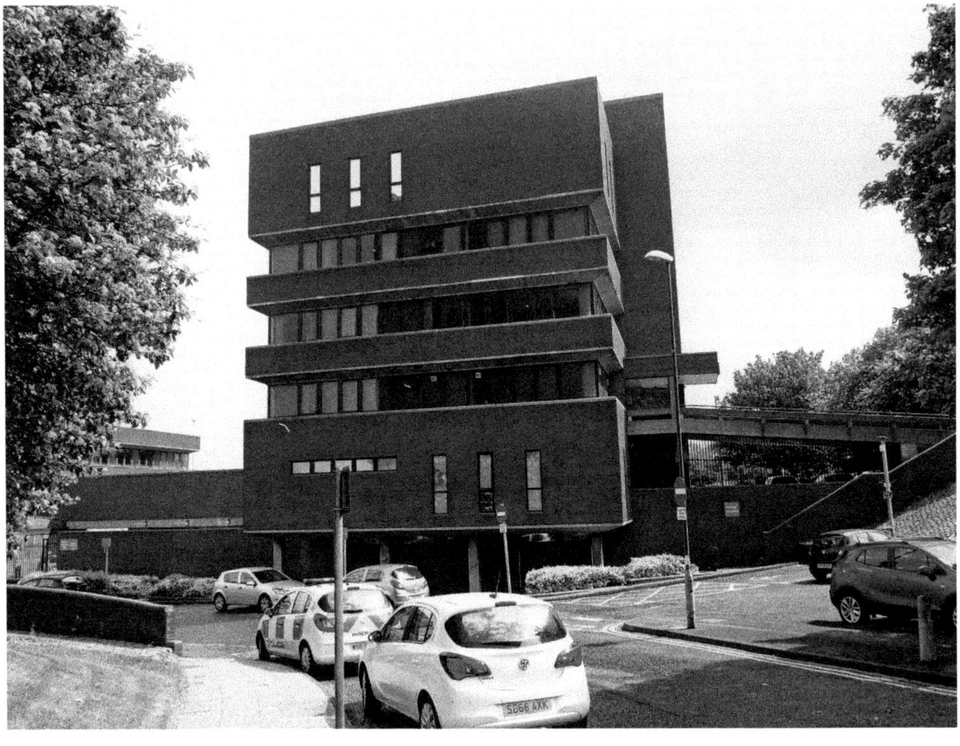

The current Gateshead police station on High West Street.

4. Ghosts and Legends

North of the river, Newcastle-upon-Tyne has a rich heritage of ghost stories and supposed haunted locations all over the city. There have been countless books written about the ghosts and ghouls of Newcastle, there's even a ghost walk, but what of Gateshead's ghostly tales?

Few people outside of Bensham will have heard the eerie tale of the 'Dead Man's Arch'. Local legend has it that a train driver caused an accident near Bensham station in which there were fatalities. Overcome with guilt, he committed suicide by hanging himself at the entrance to the footpath that runs beneath the main railway line from Elysium Terrace through to Tynevale Terrace. It's said that anyone brave, or foolish, enough to walk through the archway at midnight on New Year's Day will experience the blood-curdling terror of bumping into the lifeless, hanging corpse of the train driver. There are no dates attributed to this legend, but Bensham train station opened in 1868 and closed in 1954.

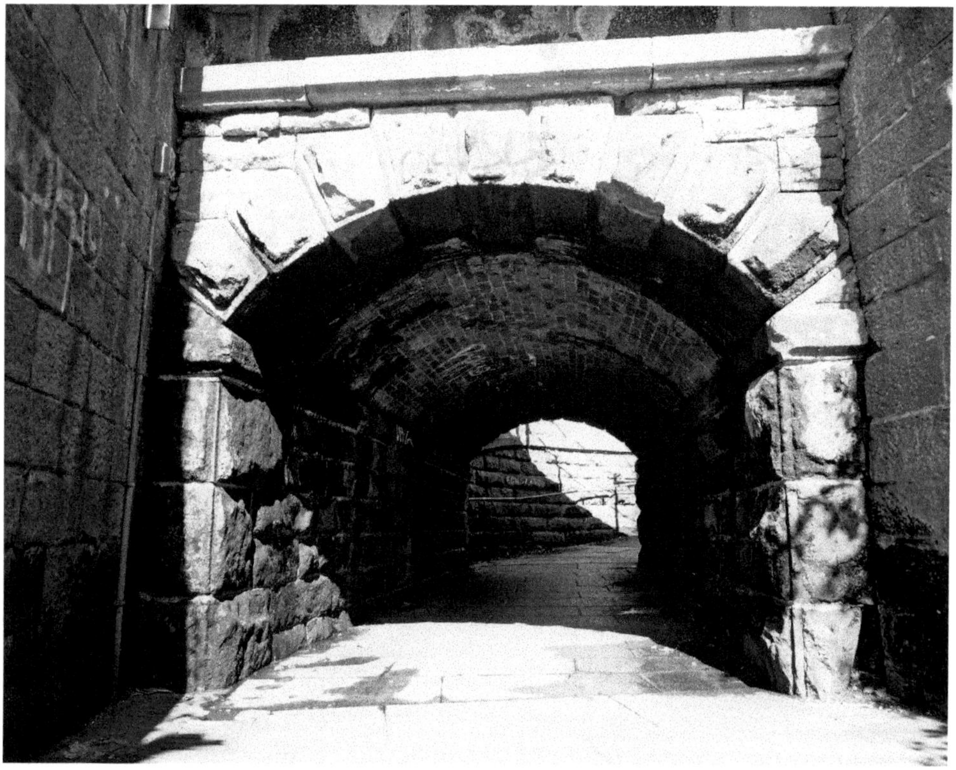

Dead Man's Arch.

Another local legend with a connection to midnight comes from Heworth. St Mary's Church has been the central point of Heworth since around AD 684, and the current church dates from 1822. The graveyard contains an ornate tomb in the unusual shape of a four-poster bed with three young children sleeping on it. It is named the Haddon Tomb as it was built by Joseph Haddon, a master mason, but it's more commonly known as 'the Babes in the Bed'. The legend goes that the three small children – George, William and their sister, whose name is lost to time as it's now illegible on the tomb – were killed in a fire after a candle fell onto the bed as they were sleeping. Joseph Haddon was their father.

It's said that if you run around the grave twelve times at the stroke of midnight, the ghostly children will appear in the darkness and play with you. This is a legend that has lasted for decades, if not centuries; however, there is a problem with it: the dates of the children's premature deaths are clearly legible on the tomb. It isn't possible that they all died in that fire as their deaths span a six-year period between 1711 and 1717 – but that's not to say the ghost story isn't true. The only way to find out would be to dare to circle the grave twelve times at midnight and see for yourself.

Next up on our tour of haunted Gateshead is a world-famous landmark that will celebrate its twentieth birthday in February 2018, and a hotel named for the 20-metre-tall sculpture that stands watch over Gateshead from its position high on a hill in Birtley.

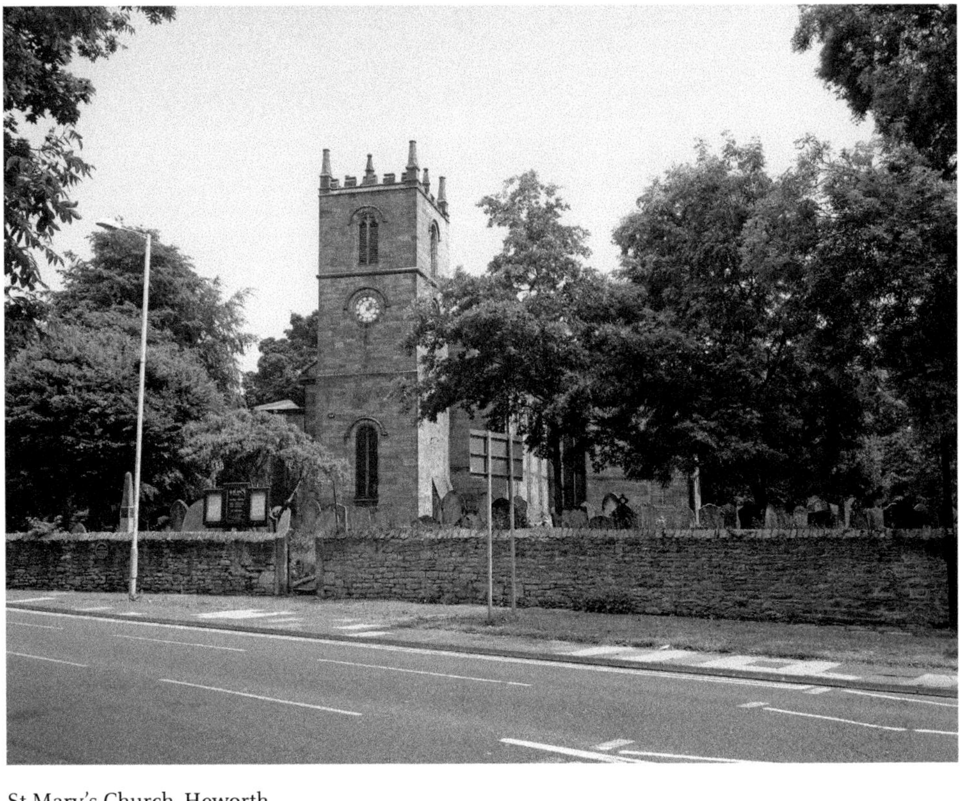

St Mary's Church, Heworth.

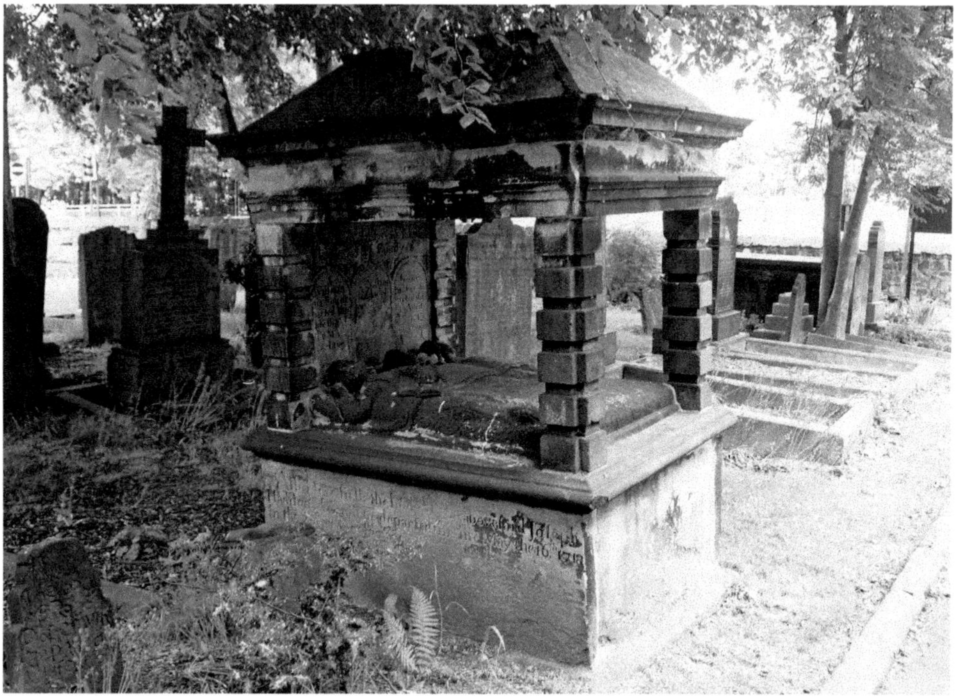

The Babes in the Bed.

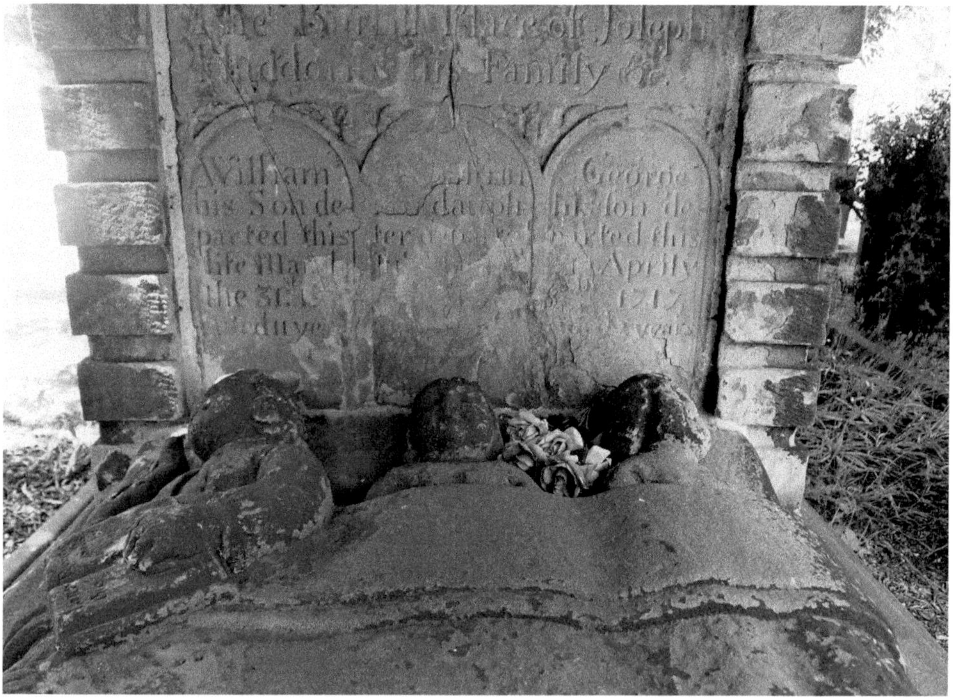

Close-up of the sleeping children of the Haddon Tomb.

The Angel View Inn was originally built as a farmhouse and stables, and the original stonework of the buildings can still be seen. Today it is a twenty-seven-bedroom hotel, restaurant, and conferencing and banqueting venue, located near to the famous sculpture for which it is named.

There is a legend of a young girl tending to a horse in the stables when the horse bolted and kicked out, hitting her in the face and killing her instantly. Is it said that she walks the corridors of the Angel View Inn; those who have seen her have described her as having a huge hole where her face should be. Staff members have also witnessed a man silently wandering the hotel – most commonly near Room 14 – and upon being approached, he vanishes.

Back in the mid-2000s a housekeeper was cleaning one of the rooms. She cleaned the bathroom and was then making the bed when she heard as noise coming from the bathroom. She tentatively entered and found that the taps on the sink and bath had all been turned fully on. A few weeks later the same housekeeper was leaving Room 15 after having cleaned it, when she noticed an imprint in the bed in the shape of a person and an imprint on the pillow where the head would be.

Late one night customers staying in Room 16 complained to staff that they were being kept awake by the sound of children noisily running and laughing outside their room. There were no children staying in the hotel that night. Guests have also reported feeling as though they aren't alone in their room, and have the unsettling sensation of being watched by unseen eyes.

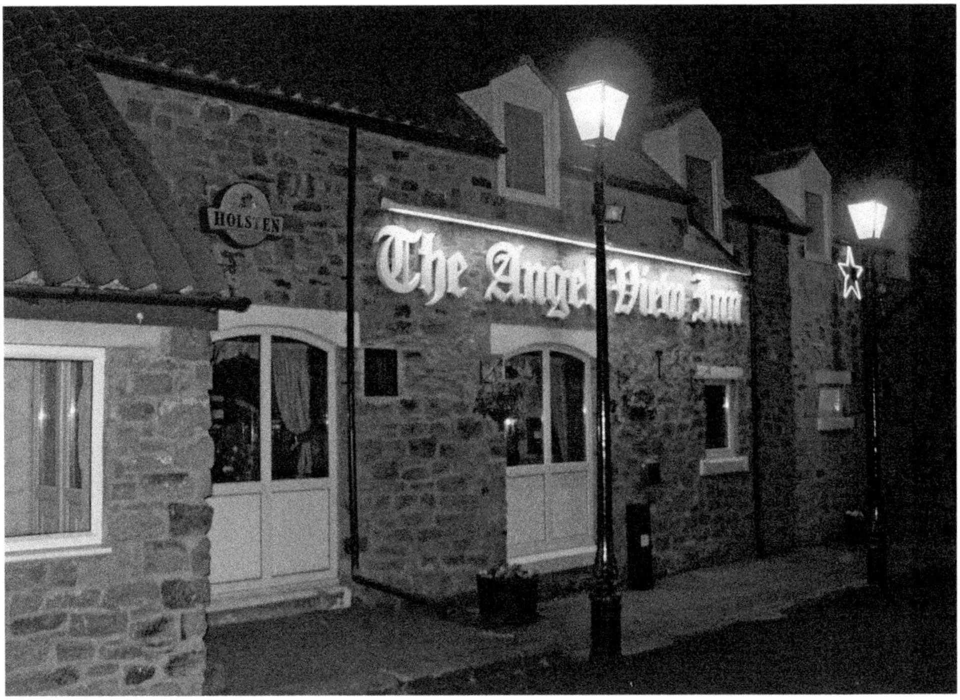

The Angel View Inn.

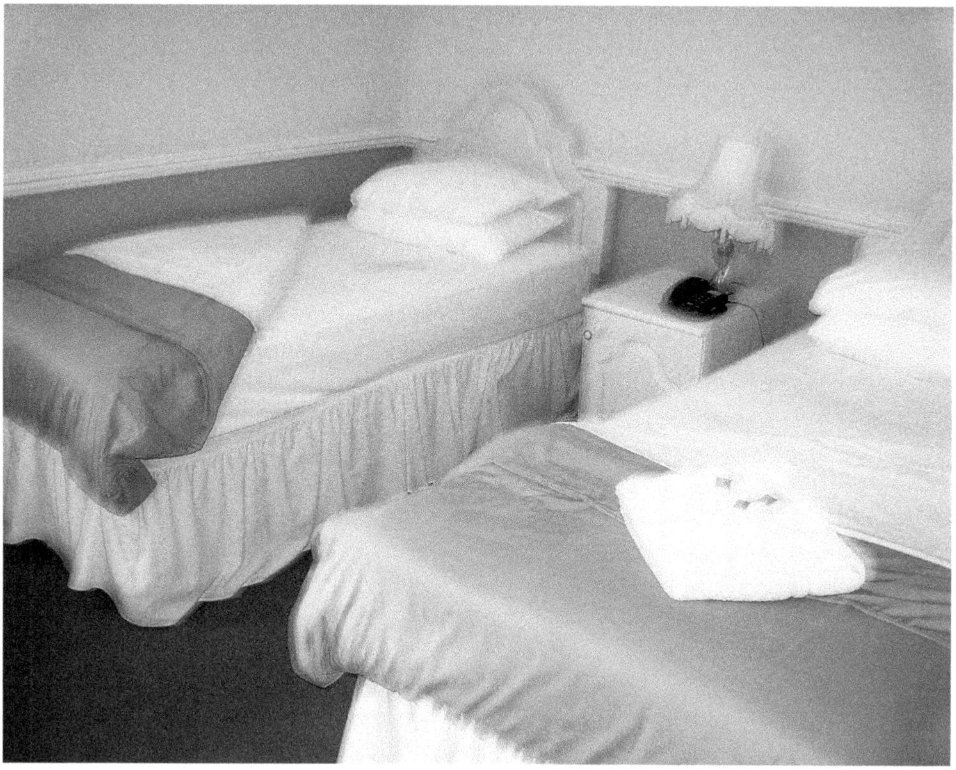

Room 14 at the Angel View Inn.

A team of paranormal investigators spent a night at the Angel View Inn back in 2005 and found evidence of poltergeist activity, including inexplicable cold spots and strange balls of light.

Back in 2008 I spent an evening in the company of Tommy Harrison, who had been night porter at the Angel View Inn for six years and had experienced some of the ghostly goings-on at the inn for himself during the many overnight shifts he had spent there.

> The previous night porter had no knowledge of the legend of the 'faceless' girl, and one night he sat down and started drawing and he drew a young girl with a dark void where her face should have been. A medium has told us that they believe the building to be haunted by six spirits ... There was one night when a woman and her two young children were staying in room 9. She awoke during the night and one of her sons was sat at the bottom of her bed. She then realised to her horror that both of her children were fast asleep and the child sat at the bottom of her bed was the ghost of a young boy ... There have been a lot of disturbances in the kitchen with pots and pans being thrown about when the room has been empty.

The Little Theatre was the only theatre in Britain built during the Second World War. It was built on a derelict site that would have housed Nos 1 and 2 Saltwell View, which were

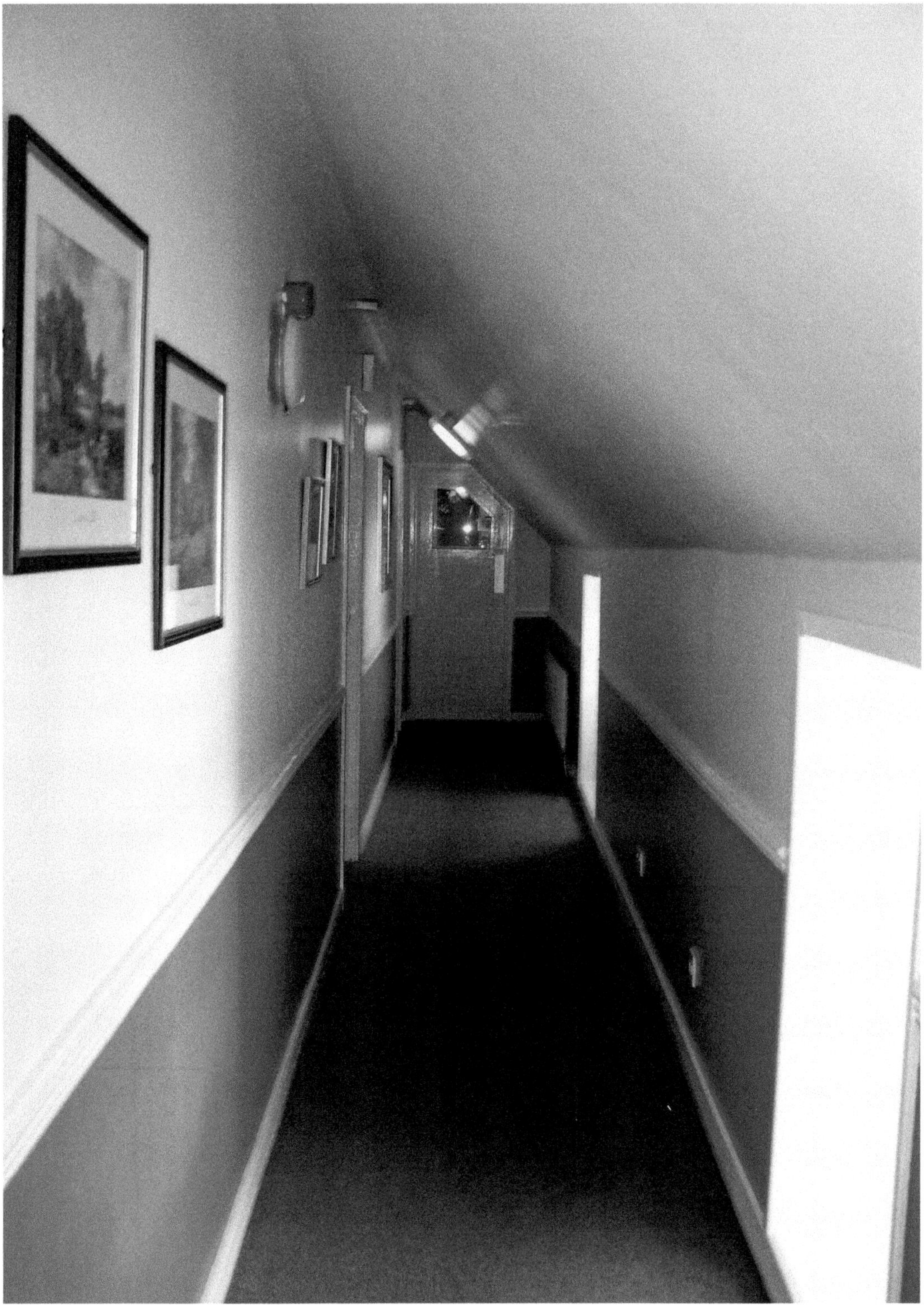

A corridor of the Angel View Inn.

purchased in 1939 thanks to the generosity of sisters Madeleine-Hope, Ruth and Sylvia Dodds of Low Fell. They were renowned public figures in the early twentieth century. Madeleine-Hope was at Cambridge before women could be awarded degrees, and would also write a book called *The Pilgrimage of Grace*, which would be considered one of the most definitive books on church history. Ruth was a prominent Labour politician in Gateshead during the 1930s and would become an honorary freeman of Gateshead in 1965.

Building a theatre during hostilities led to a number of interruptions; at one point it was requisitioned as a barrage balloon station, and on another occasion a bomb fell on nearby Saltwell Park, blowing out the windows and doors of the theatre. With the theatre finally ready to put on shows for the people of Gateshead, the opening performance was of *A Midsummer Night's Dream* on 13 October 1943.

No. 3 Saltwell View came up for sale was purchased and incorporated into the new building immediately. The Little Theatre and the Progressive Players, a repertory company formed in 1920 who frequently performed at the Little Theatre once it opened, went from strength to strength. During the 1960s and 1970s things began to look bleak for the theatre: the threat of demolition hung over the building to make way for a new road, though, thankfully, this never came to be. In 1989, No. 4 was purchased to ease overcrowding and allow further expansion. In recent years the building, which is now Gateshead's only theatre, has undergone a major facelift, which was completed by late 2013 in time for the building's seventieth birthday.

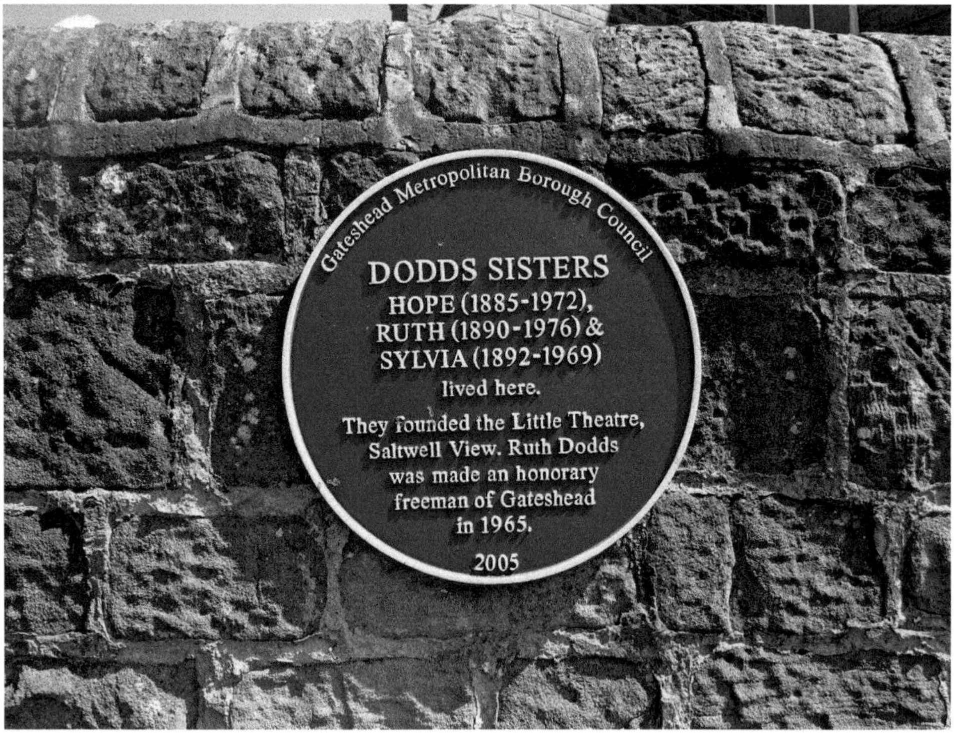

Dodds Sisters' blue plaque at Home House, Low Fell.

Another thing that has happened in recent years to the Little Theatre is its growing reputation as one of the north-east's haunted hotspots, with groups from far and wide conducting paranormal investigations at the theatre. Spectral figures have been seen in the changing rooms and walking the corridors of the building. At times, when the stage has been completely empty, people have clearly heard footsteps walking across it. People have heard whispering in their ear when they've been alone too. Why this unassuming, still relatively young theatre should have phantom residents is unclear, but as these paranormal investigations continue perhaps we'll get closer to discovering what secrets the building holds.

Gateshead hit the headlines in June 1964 when children playing on the Leam Lane Estate claimed to have encountered the arrival of little green men from another world. The *Newcastle Journal* reported on 9 June that a week earlier on the 2nd, four boys had been playing, and at 4.10 p.m. they spotted 'a silver domed object about the size of a table, with portholes around the top and three legs. It was seen falling like a leaf through the sky making a low buzzing noise descending approximately 120 yards away from where they were standing'.

Another report arrived at 5.30 p.m. when David Wilson, fourteen years old, walked down to the farm to collect some straw for his rabbits and was confused to find a group of around ten children excitedly stood around a haystack. When he got closer he was astonished to see 'around six to eight tiny human beings on top of the stack: they were

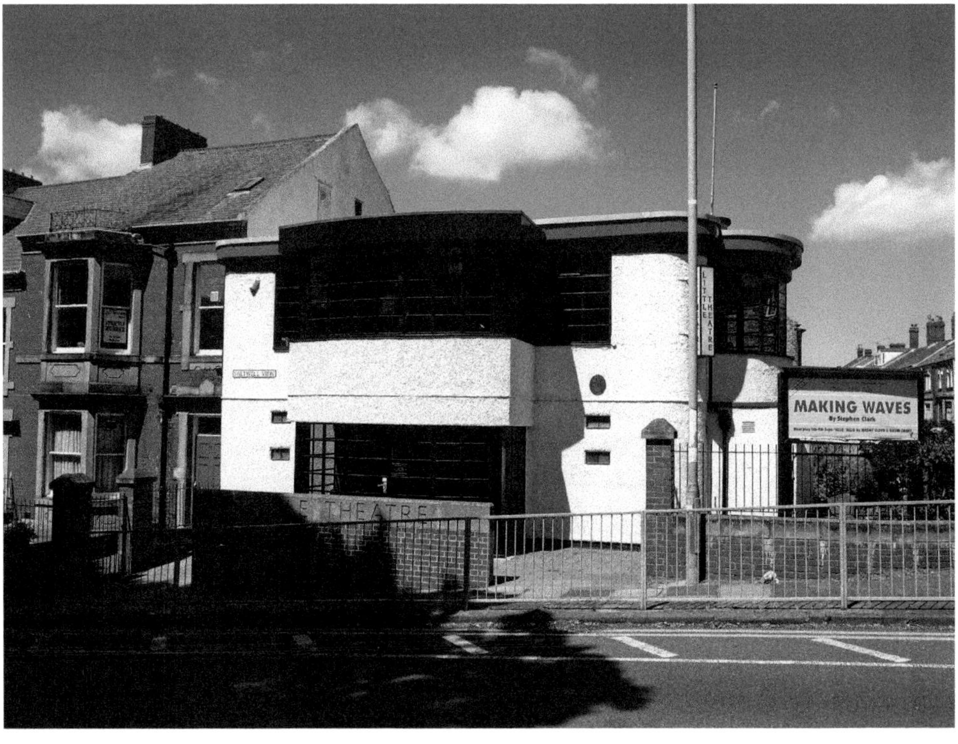

The Little Theatre.

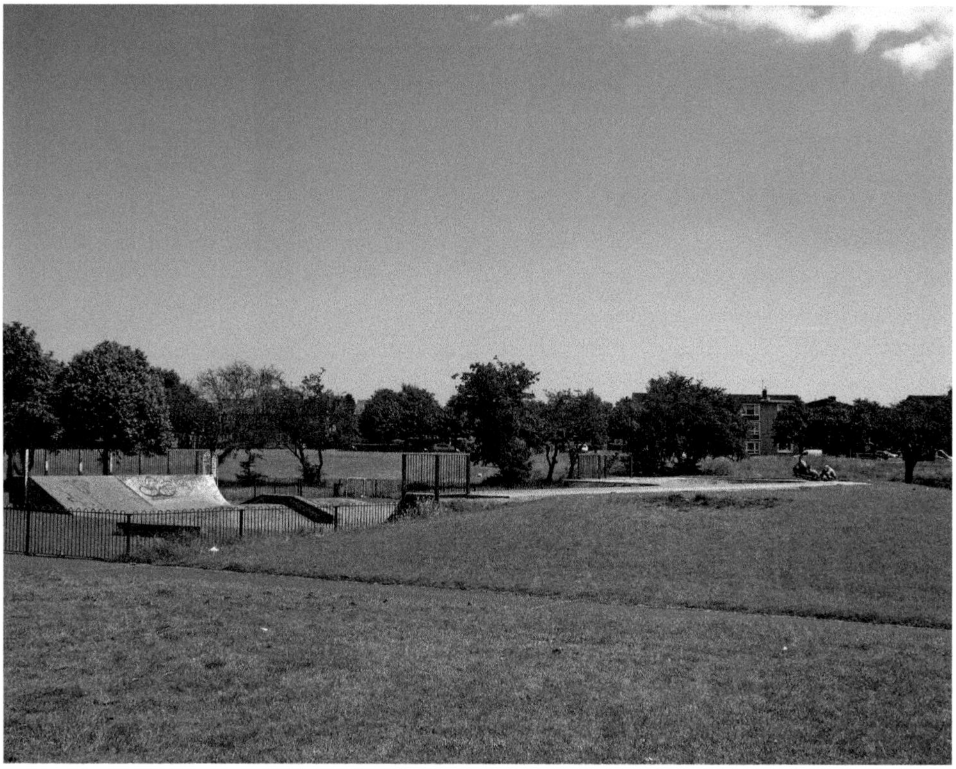

The Leam Lane Estate, unrecognisable since the alien invasion of 1964.

about two feet tall and dressed in bright green suits. They appeared to be digging into the haystack, as if searching for something. Their hands were lit up like electric light bulbs.'

A girl at the scene told the newspaper she had seen a circular silvery object take off from the ground with a spinning motion and giving off an orange glow. Another said 'the leader of the little green men was dressed in black and carried a baton with pink stripes,' while another added that 'he was sitting on the roof of the barn watching us.' The children said that the leader was riding around on the back of a cow.

The farmer who owned the land that this was reported to have happened on didn't believe a word of it and said, 'All these claims are a load of nonsense. If anything has landed I would've known about it. I have a dog kept in the yard, he would have warned me if anybody had been prowling around the farm.'

Interestingly, in the December 1964 issue of the American paranormal magazine *Ray Palmer's Flying Saucers*, an article was written about a separate incident that occurred at 11.35 p.m. on 31 May 1964. The Bell family, who lived on the Leam Lane Estate, saw three egg-shaped luminous flashes pass east to west through the sky, which were visible for 'around three seconds'. Many of their neighbours were awoken by a strange humming noise that started at 12.30 a.m. on the same night and lasted until around 1 a.m. It was described as being 'like a swarm of bees but twenty times louder'. The family's thirteen-year-old son, Keith Bell, wondered if it could have been related to another incident from a few days earlier, when a silver disk had been seen hovering above the nearby farm at around midday on 28 May.

Another truly astonishing report of an alien encounter dates back to the Second World War, when one of these extra-terrestrial beings learnt the hard way not to mess with a Geordie lad. In the spring of 1940, five-year-old Robert Hall was playing with friends in Bensham, watching in fascination at soldiers marching along Saltwell Road. It was getting cold so he headed home, but encountered an unusual 'blur' in the street, which stopped them seeing what was behind it. They walked through it and were terrified with what greeted them: an egg-shaped spacecraft with around twenty aliens. He described most of them as horrible-looking 2–4-feet-tall aliens, which resembled the 'greys' that we think of these days as typical aliens. Three of them were different: one looked like Bigfoot and another was wearing a strange helmet similar to modern-day astronaut helmets but filled with some kind of liquid; the final one looked just like a very tall man, with long flowing blonde hair and wearing a cape.

The aliens spoke perfect English – but with no hint of an accent – and told Robert that they were going to examine him. The terrified boy had no choice but to comply. The aliens then said they were going to extract some blood from his neck and added that if he moved during the procedure, he would die. By now a group of girls had also stumbled onto the scene; they were petrified and ran for their lives. They tried to climb over a barbed wire fence to the railway line but caught their skin on the barbed wire, screaming and crying. A black dog with the alien creatures approached the girls as if to attack, however Robert grabbed a wand-type device from the belt of one of the aliens and fired a beam of light at the dog, sedating it immediately.

DID YOU KNOW?

It is interesting that the Angel of the North itself is believed to be haunted by a phantom Second World War Nazi recruitment officer. A number of visitors to the Antony Gormley sculpture have reported seeing the phantom, most commonly in the twilight, just after the last traces of sunlight have faded away beyond the horizon.

The whole incident lasted around twenty minutes, and then Robert and his friend were allowed to leave. They ran and found a nearby soldier. They told him their fanciful tale and he said 'it'll just be some kids messing around', but they persuaded the soldier to take a look. As they returned to the aliens they spotted a UFO taking off. The soldier opened fire, drawing attention to the otherworldly craft, and the street was in chaos as people fled from the gunfire. Robert claims that hundreds of witnesses must have seen the object take flight and disappear into the sky.

When Robert got home he told his parents, but, a five-year-old boy telling tales of aliens and spaceships, of course they didn't believe him. However, the next day two men in black suits came to his house and warned Robert that if he was to tell anyone what had happened the previous day he would disappear.

A few days later, Robert was walking down the street and one of the 'horrible-looking' grey aliens appeared and tried to grab him. It was on him in seconds and Robert fell over the kerb trying to get away, bashing his toe. Thankfully for Robert, his Uncle Ernie, who lived nearby, saw what was happening to his nephew, grabbed a coal shovel and smashed the would-be abductor in the face with it. The creature lay still on the floor; it was dead.

Robert was sent to find a local policeman, Sergeant Brookes from Saltwell Road. When the young lad found Sergeant Brooks he said, 'he's killed it, he's killed it'. The policeman assumed there'd been a murder and reached for his truncheon, but Robert told him to follow him. When the policeman saw the alien he started crossing himself and praying, then helped Ernie put the body inside a coal sack. Twenty minutes later the alien was loaded into a car and taken half a mile away to St Cuthbert's Church on Bensham Road, where it could be hidden. Robert saw the coal sack taken to the back of the church, where some steps led beneath the church and out of sight. It remained hidden beneath the church for three months.

The following day Robert saw men come to the church wearing white coats and carrying little suitcases. After going under the church for some time they went door to door in the streets – near where the initial alien encounter occurred – and searched each house, looking for any other grey aliens who may have remained after the ship flew off a few days earlier.

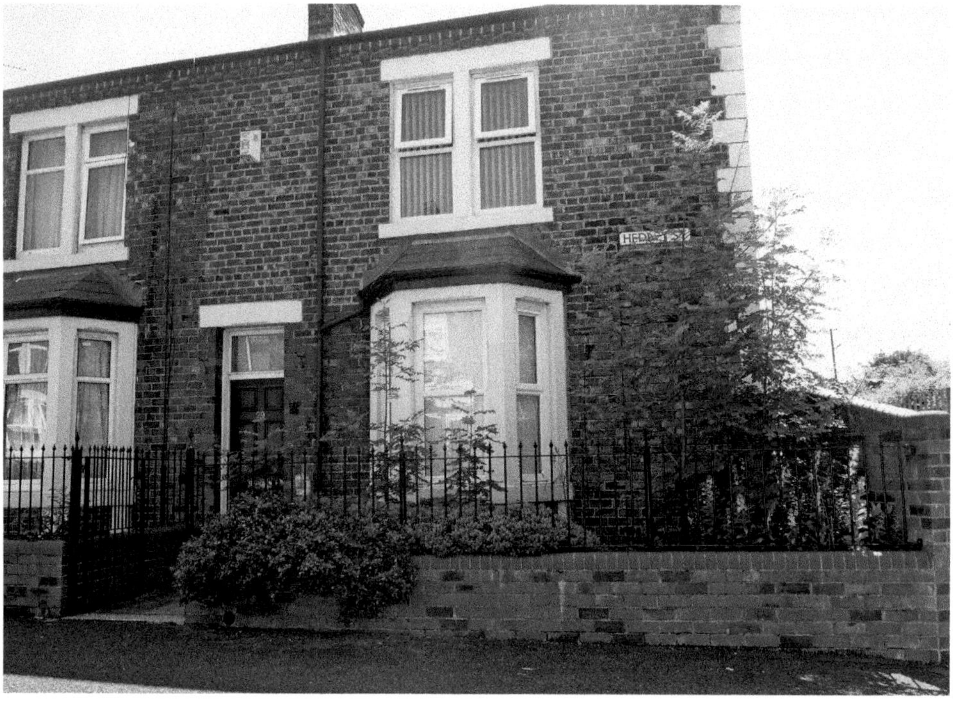

No. 29 Hedley Street, once home to Robert Hall. Men in black visited him here.

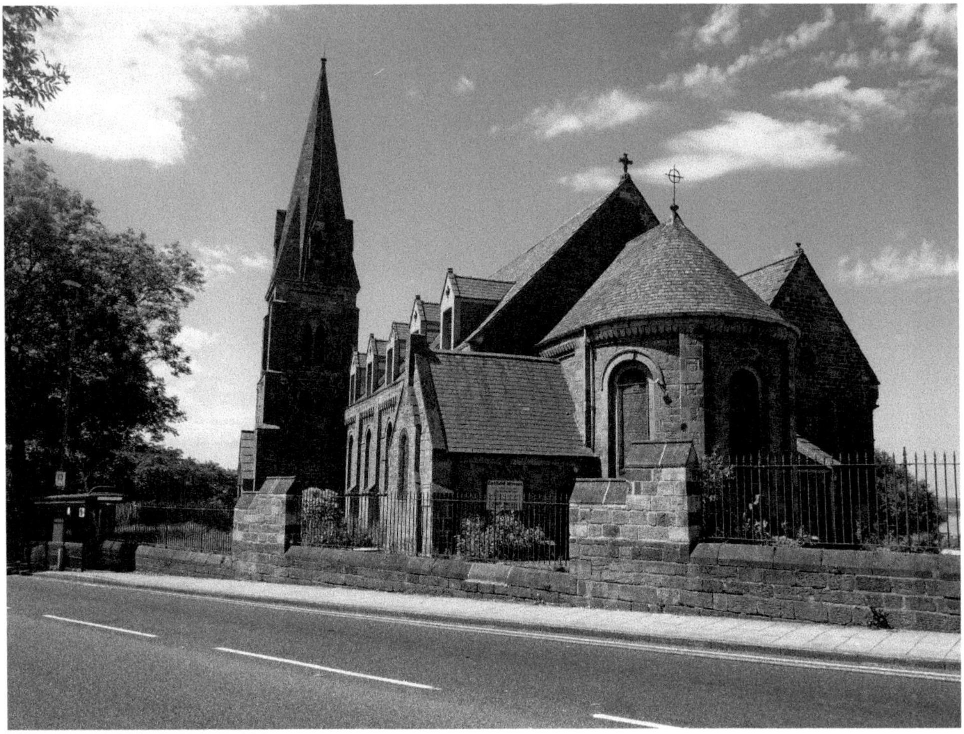

St Cuthbert's Church, Bensham. Was an alien corpse hidden here in 1940?

Robert says that strange, small triangular marks appeared on his left cheek, where they remained until he was around twelve or thirteen before disappearing without a trace.

In 2011, Robert, aged seventy-six, talked to the *Northern Echo* as his incredible story had become the subject of a television documentary. He added that he has been the subject of ridicule ever since the incident over seventy years earlier: 'At school the teacher would say "there's the boy who believes in little green men". They weren't bloody green, they were grey. I will take it to my grave.'

I visited St Cuthbert's Church in the summer of 2017, the very location where seventy-seven years earlier a dead alien body was said to be have been hidden. The church is closed down and is in the process of being converted into a museum. Sadly, the stairs the alien corpse was taken down have been destroyed as part of this modernisation, meaning the room where the body was stored is now inaccessible.

5. Wartime

On 23 January 1900 over forty brave Gateshead men were sworn into the 5th Battalion of the Durham Light Infantry (DLI) to fight in the Boer War. Over 280 applied, but Colonel Proctor, who officiated over the ceremony, was said to have selected 'as good a body of men as that would see the whole corps, who would be a credit to their country'.

These men were welcomed with a lavish dinner and a smoking concert at the drill hall in Bensham. These concerts were hugely popular during Victorian times, where only men were allowed to attend and they would smoke and chat while listening to live music.

After this ceremony they marched in full uniform, complete with their newly allocated rifles. They were cheered every step by the Gateshead residents who had lined the streets, despite the awful winter weather, to greet their very own local heroes. They sang and chanted until they reached the Town Hall, where a platform had been erected to swear the soldiers in.

Gateshead has two memorials to commemorate the courage of those men who lost their lives during the Boer War (1899–1902); they are in Saltwell Park and on Durham Road in Low Fell.

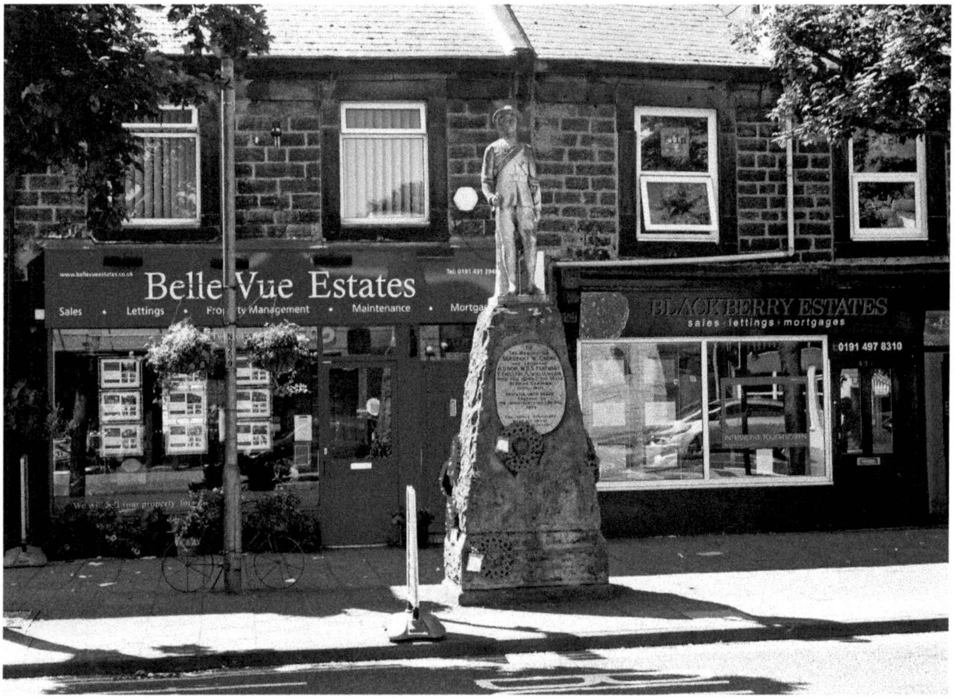

Boer War memorial in Low Fell in 2017.

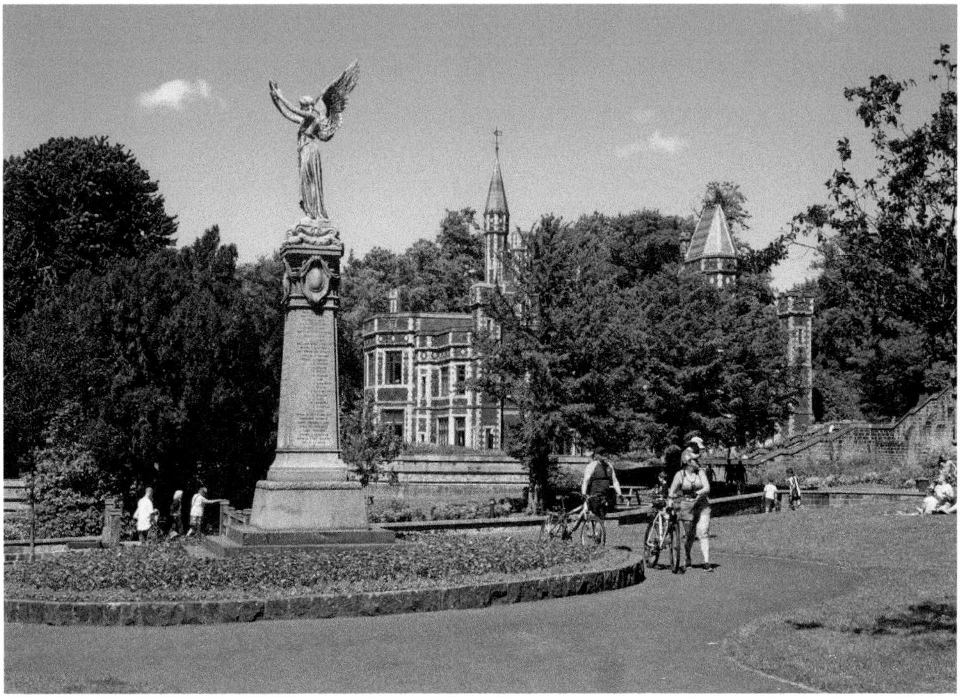

Boer War memorial in Saltwell Park.

When the United Kingdom entered in the First World War on 4 August 1914, the men of Gateshead, as with the men across all of Britain, were placed under huge pressure to enlist and do their duty for king and country. Recruiting offices were opened across the town on the High Street, at the Town Hall, and at a number of drill halls. Around 20,000 Gateshead men joined the war effort, enlisting for one of the armed forces and leaving their loved ones behind. Most signed up for the Durham Light Infantry, with others joining the Tyneside Irish, Tyneside Scottish or the Northumberland Fusiliers.

It has been claimed that the first shot fired by a Brit in the war was by a Gateshead man. John Brown-King of Windy Nook was aboard HMS *Amphion*, an Active-class scout cruiser, which was patrolling the North Sea on 5 August – the first full day of Britain's involvement in the war. Early in the morning the *Amphion* encountered the SMS *Königin Luise*, a former Hamburg–Holland ferry that had been converted into a German minelayer and was in the process of dropping mines just off the Thames Estuary. It is believed that Brown-King fired the first shot at the enemy ship, sinking it and securing the Royal Navy their first victory of the war.

In a cruel twist of fate, the following day the *Amphion* would become the first British ship lost in the war when it struck one of the mines dropped so recently by the *Königin Luise*. The explosion ripped the ship apart and many of the men, including prisoners rescued from the wreckage of the German minelayer, were killed in the initial blast. Brown-King was hospitalised at the Shotley Naval Hospital in Harwick, but died on 23 August from the wounds he had sustained.

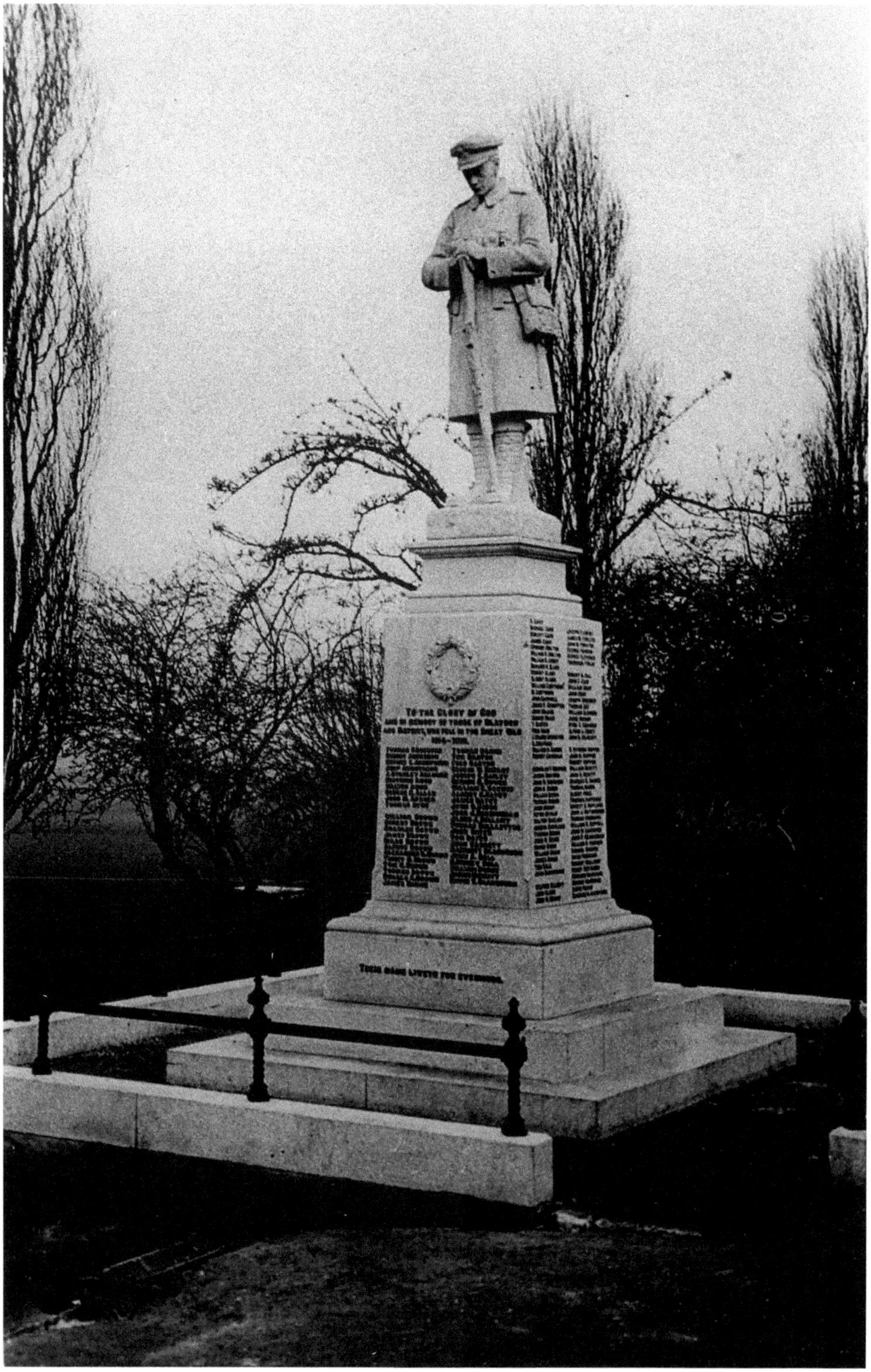

First World War memorial in Blaydon, unveiled in 1923. (Photo courtesy of Gateshead Libraries)

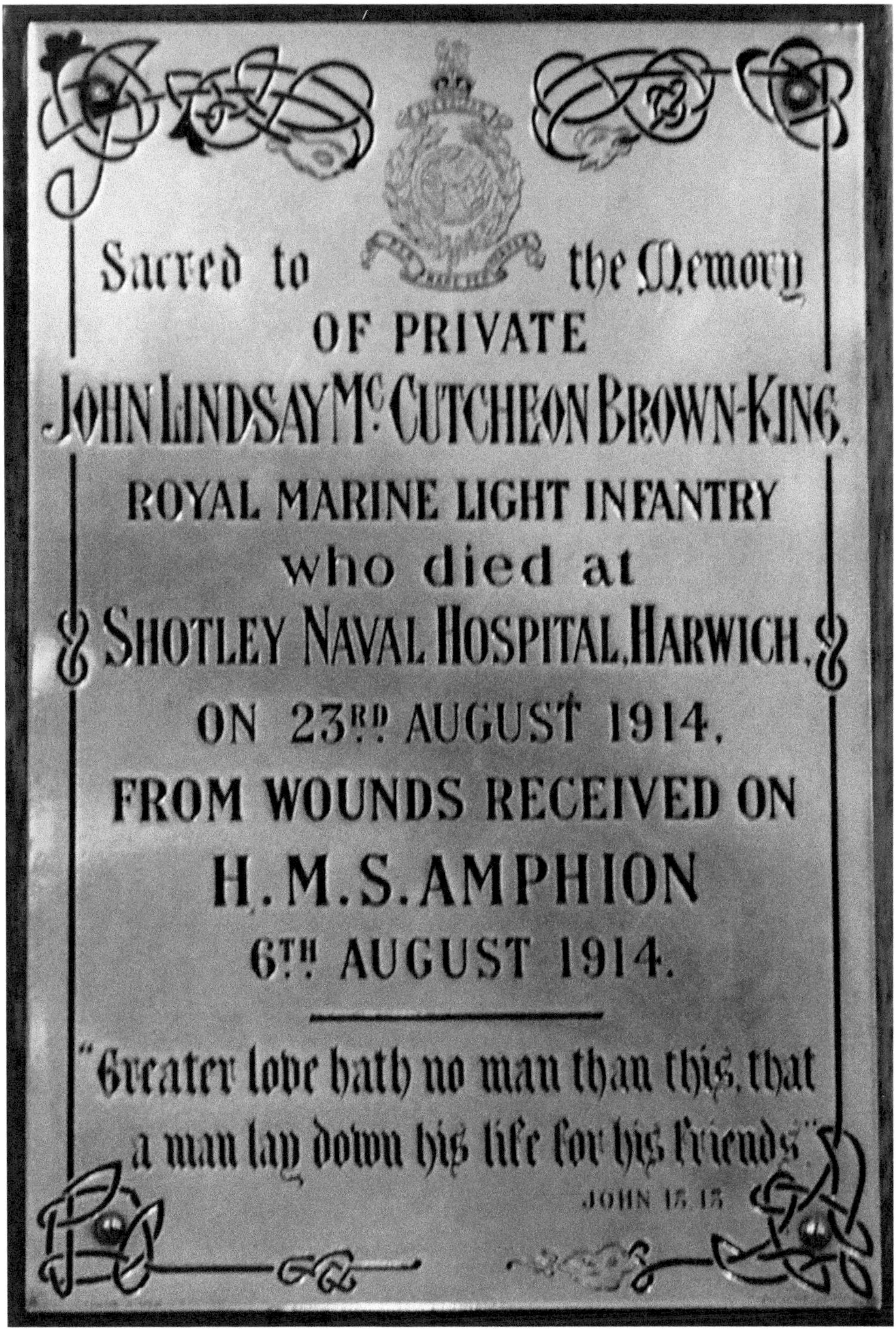

John Brown-King memorial at St Alban's Church, Windy Nook.

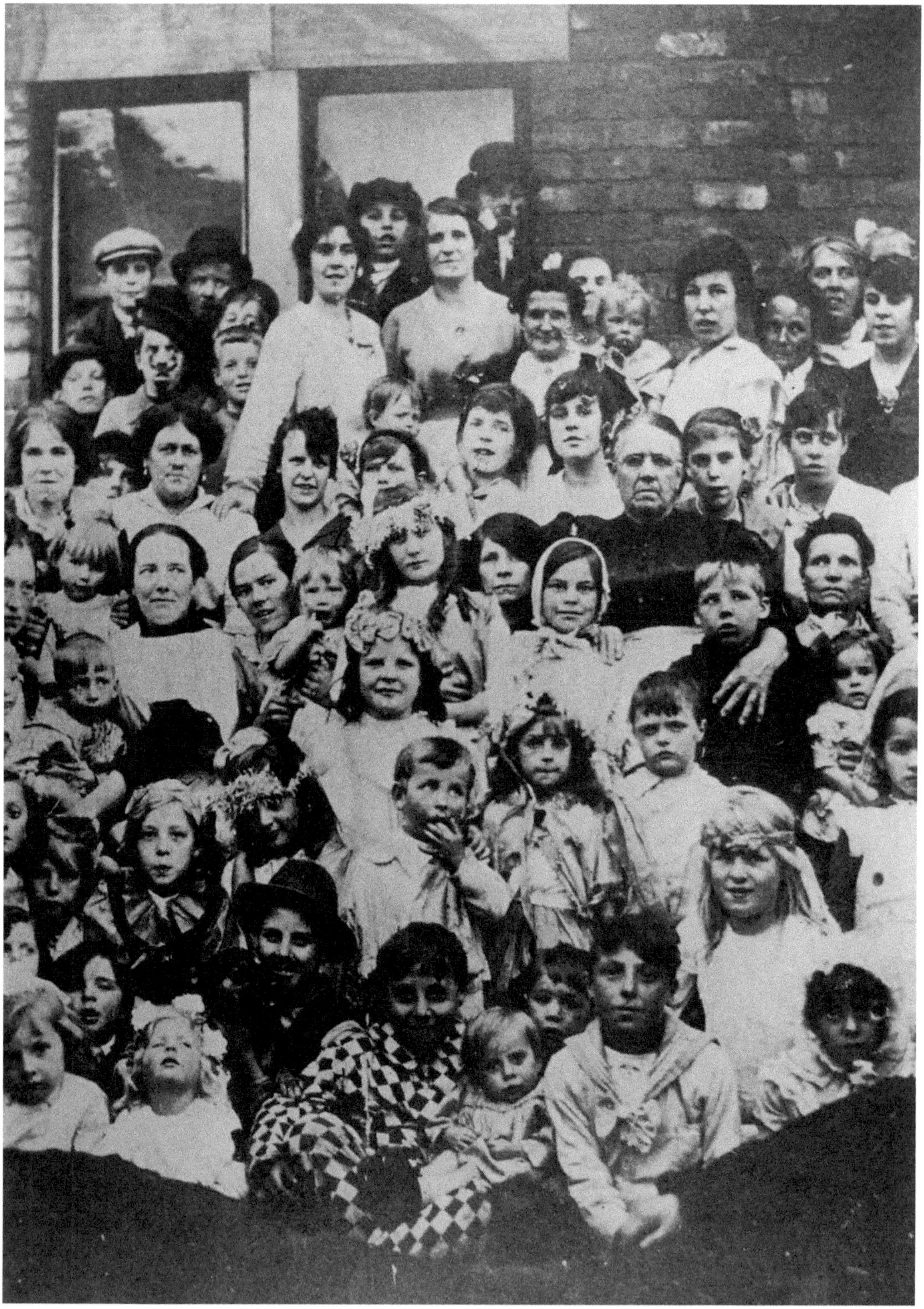

Armastice street party, Blaydon 1918. (Photo courtesy of Gateshead Libraries)

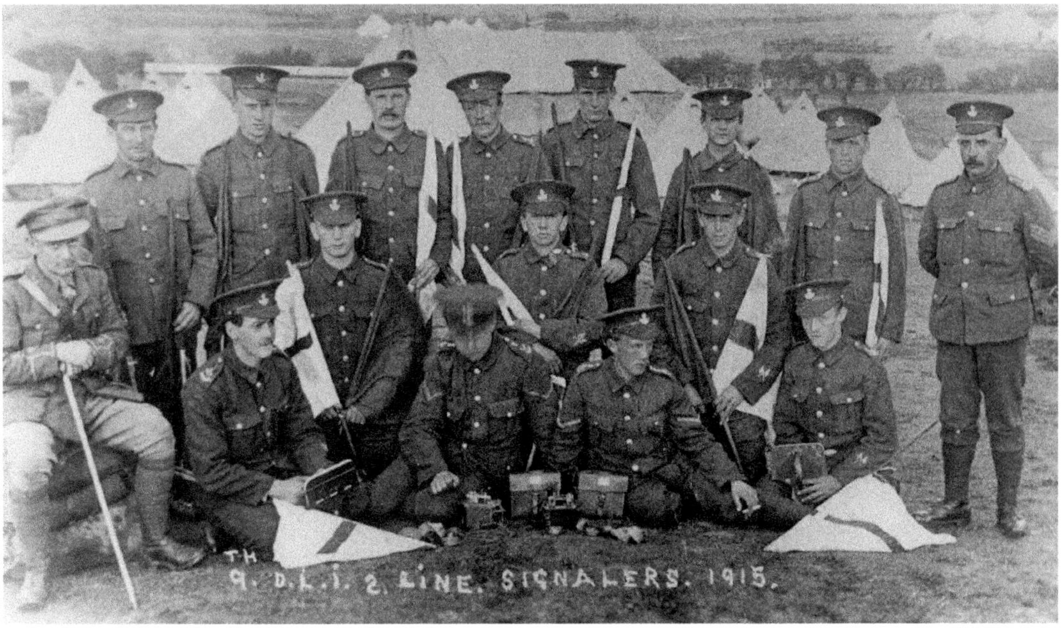

The 9th Durham Light Infantry in 1915. (Photo courtesy of Gateshead Libraries)

The loss of life was horrendous. Over 9 million military personal died in battle worldwide, and over 7 million civilians were killed. Of the UK's 6 million men who were called up, over 700,000 were killed; included in that figure were over 1,700 Gateshead men who left for war but would never return home. Many of those who did make it back to their families and friends returned a shadow of their former selves. Many were maimed – physically or mentally – as a result of what they had endured in those four long years of hell. The 9th Battalion of the Durham Light Infantry were awarded more individual medals than any other unit in the British army, but they also sustained terrible losses.

In the wake of the war, monuments and memorials honouring the fallen were built the length and breadth of Britain. No less than twelve war memorials were erected across Gateshead, such was the tragic loss, yet immense pride, felt by the town.

On 14 May 1922 thousands turned out to the opening of an ornate cenotaph on the corner of Prince Consort Road and Durham Road, a ceremony overseen by the Bishop of Durham. It is one of the most ambitious memorials in the region, with the bronze figure of a warrior with an unsheathed sword ready for battle, flanked by Grecian Ionic pillars. Below the figure, at the top of the three stone steps, is a beautifully decorated door made of teak, leading to a chamber. This room was host to a stone lectern holding the book of remembrance, behind the lectern is a curved wall featuring an inscription, and above it hanging an ever burning lamp in memory of the fallen. The book was a roll of honour of those brave Gateshead men who were lost to war, most of those in attendance will have lost husbands, brothers, fathers, sons and friends, whose names will have featured on those pages. The roll of honour would later be moved to the nearby library for safekeeping.

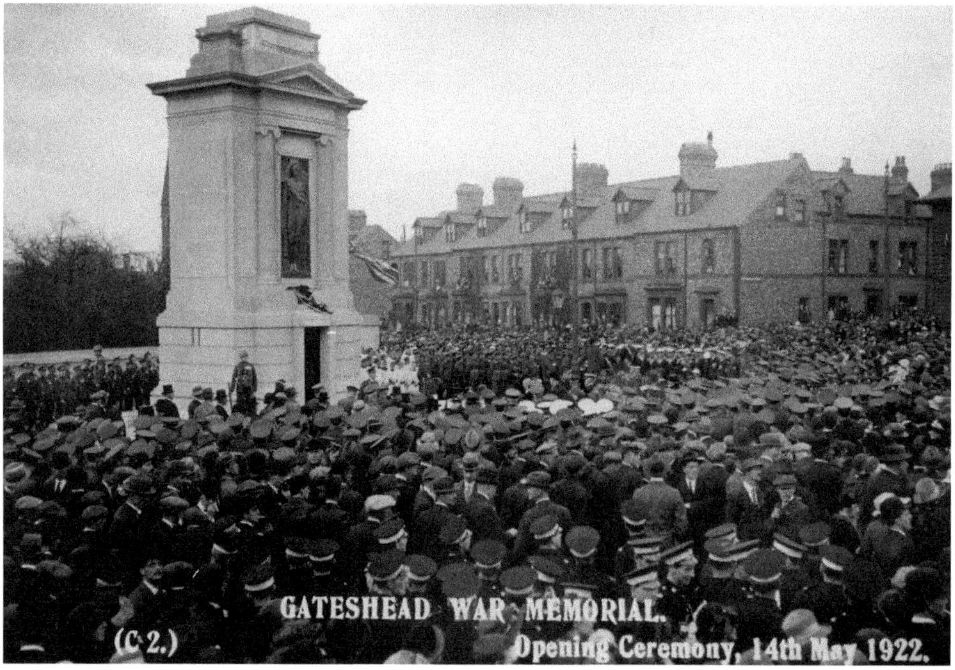

Opening of First World War memorial on Prince Consort Road 1922. (Photo courtesy of Gateshead Libraries)

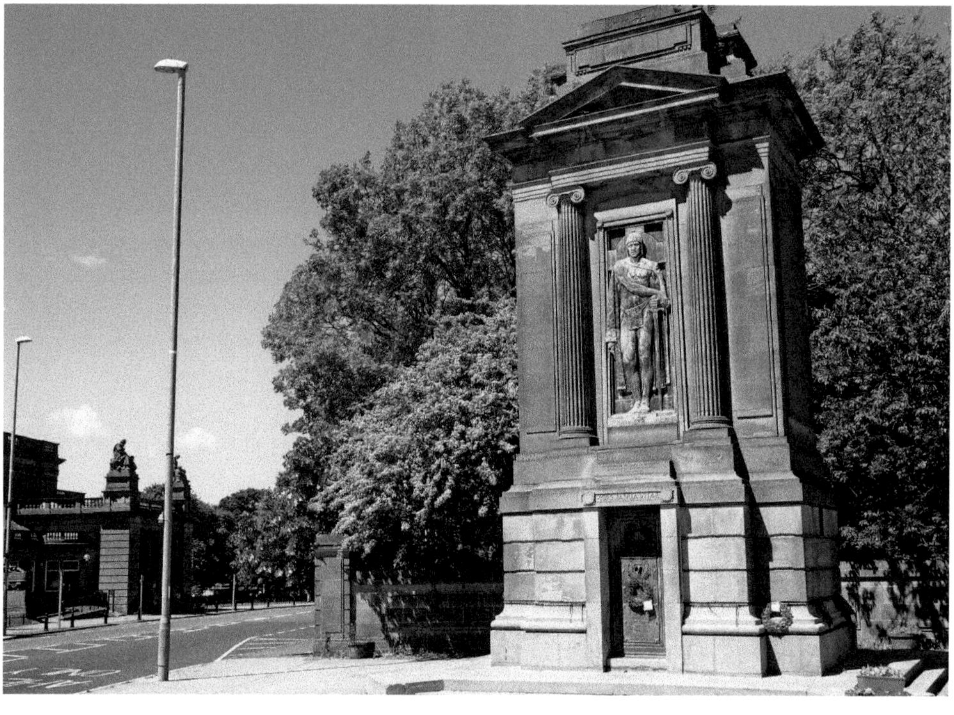

First World War memorial on Prince Consort Road in the summer of 2017.

On 1 September 1939 Germany invaded Poland. On the morning of the 3rd the British government gave Adolf Hitler an ultimatum: withdraw your troops from Poland by 11 a.m. or they would send forces. Germany didn't respond, nor did they withdraw their troops. Prime Minister Neville Chamberlain announced to the nation on BBC radio that as of 11.15 a.m. on 3 September 1939, Britain were once more at war with Germany.

Across the rest of the year recruitment drives were held across Britain, and Gateshead men were once again being encouraged to enlist and serve their country. All men between the age of eighteen and forty-one were made to register for service as the National Service (Armed Forces) Act had been enacted by Parliament on the day war was declared. Those medically unfit were exempt, as were others in key industries such as engineering, baking, farming and medicine.

Such was the threat of German bombers, air-raid shelters were built across the town. In August 1939, a plan was also being drawn up to evacuate children to safer areas of the country – mostly to north Yorkshire – separated from their family and friends and placed into families to be taken care of until it was deemed safe to return home. All too soon there was a real need to evacuate these children. Full-scale rehearsals took place on Monday 28 August, with thousands of children assembled in schoolyards across the town clutching a few personal possessions, a box containing a gas mask, and a label secured to their clothing bearing their name.

Across 1 and 2 September 'Operation Pied Piper' saw almost 3 million evacuees relocated, with 10,598 children evacuated from Gateshead. This was 71 per cent of the children eligible to be moved for their own safety. Understandably, many parents didn't want to be separated from their children and stayed home to face whatever dangers the Germans had in store alongside their family.

Before long it was an all too common sight to see German bombers flying in along the Tyne from the entrance to the river from the North Sea towards Newcastle; the Luftwaffe (German Air Force) dropping bombs attempting to hit the factories and shipyards along the river. Royal artillery guns were positioned on both sides of the river to attempt to shoot down the bombers bearing the swastika before they could do any substantial damage. Barrage balloons were also strategically positioned along the Tyne flying on metal cables, in the hope the cable would catch the plane, damaging a wing or cutting of a propeller, causing it to crash.

DID YOU KNOW?

During the Second World War the people of Gateshead raised the £10,000 needed to fund the Gateshead Spitfire to defend the country, and it flew with a Gateshead crest.

During 1940 and 1941 was the Blitz – from the German word *Blitzkrieg*, meaning 'Lightning War' – this was Germany's campaign of sustained aerial bombing, which lasted

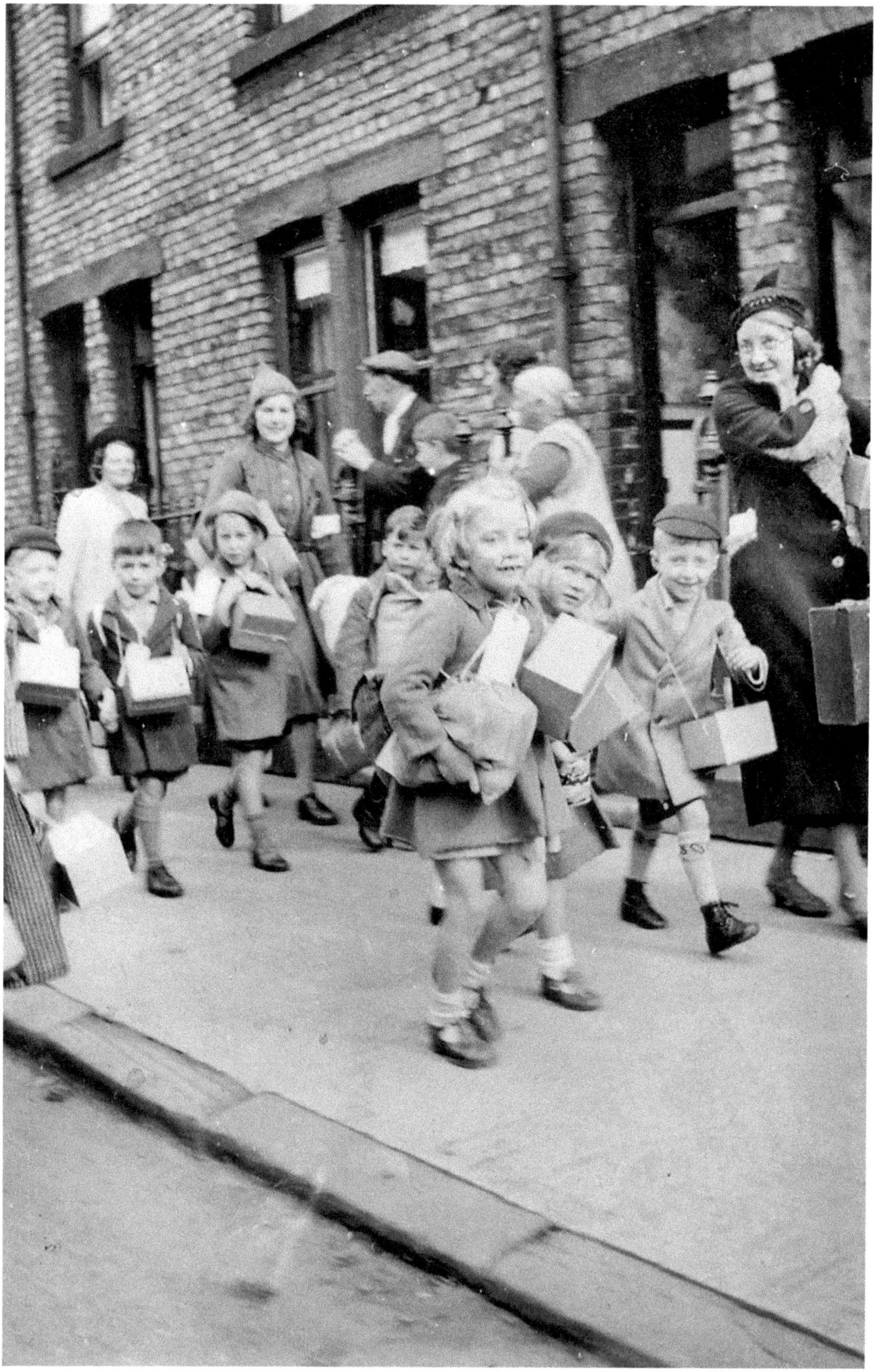

Evacuation of schoolchildren in 1939. (Photo courtesy of Gateshead Libraries)

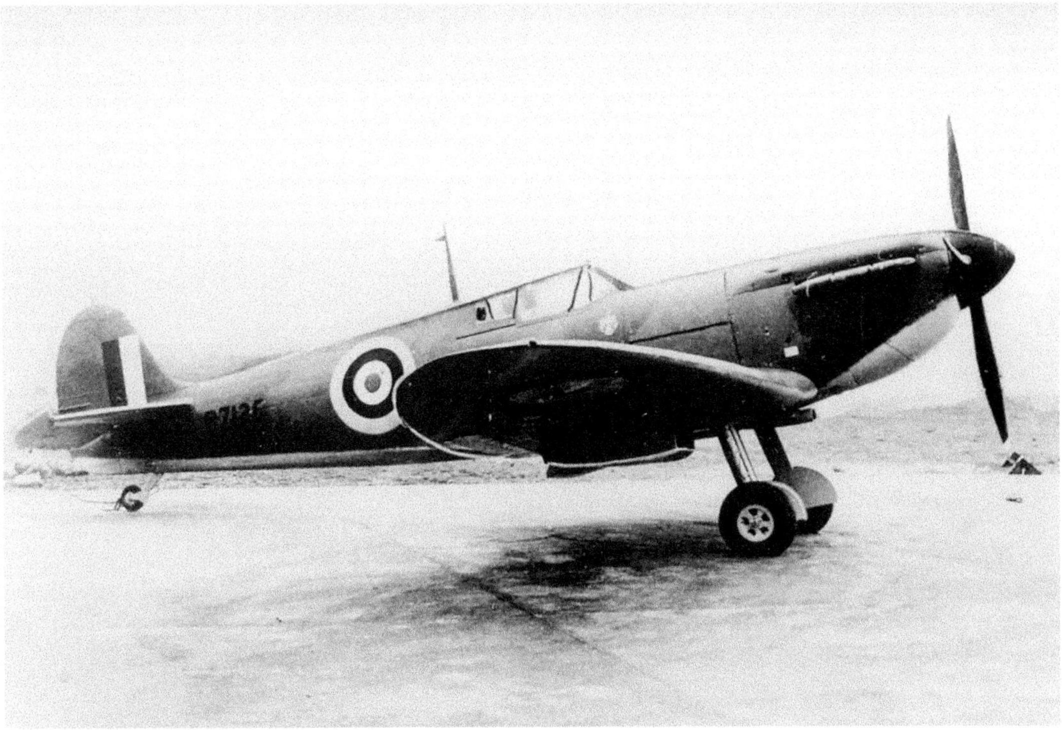

The Gateshead Spitfire in 1939. (Photo courtesy of Gateshead Libraries)

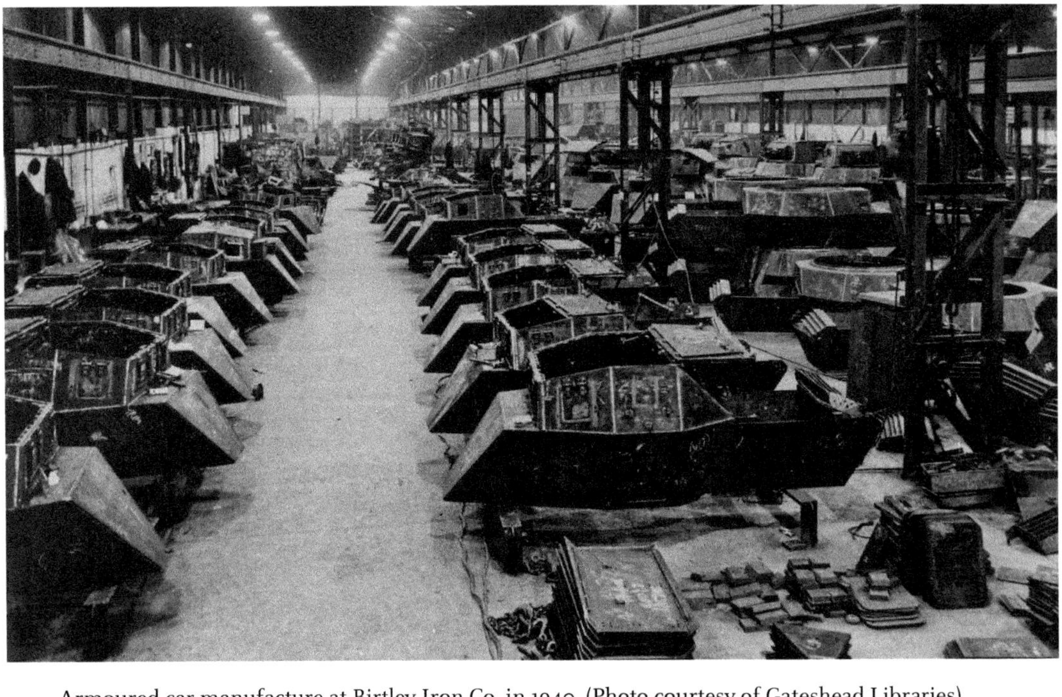

Armoured car manufacture at Birtley Iron Co. in 1940. (Photo courtesy of Gateshead Libraries)

eight months and claimed the lives of 43,000 civilians. Gateshead was fortunate in that only five people lost their lives in these bombing raids as the majority of the bombs fell within the grounds of Saltwell Park.

With most young men away at war Britain faced a severe labour shortage, and on 18 December 1941 the National Service Act (No. 2) was passed by Parliament. This saw all unmarried women aged between twenty and thirty (later extended to nineteen to forty-three) join the armed forces, work in a factory or work on the land with the Women's Land Army. This was later extended to include married women, although pregnant women and mothers with young children were exempt from this work. By mid-1943 around 90 per cent of single women and 80 per cent of married women were employed in work considered vital to the war effort.

One vital need was for women to work in munitions factories. Other women were conscripted to work in tank and aircraft factories, civil defence, nursing, transport and other key occupations, even driving trains and operating anti-aircraft guns. Important jobs in Gateshead were working with gas and tar – hard work that had previously been seen as 'men's work'.

The year 1945 finally saw the war come to an end and street parties were held throughout Gateshead as the town's people celebrated peace; however, many loved ones were lost, and with rationing in place until June 1954 it would be a long time before things would begin to seem normal once again as Britain rebuilt.

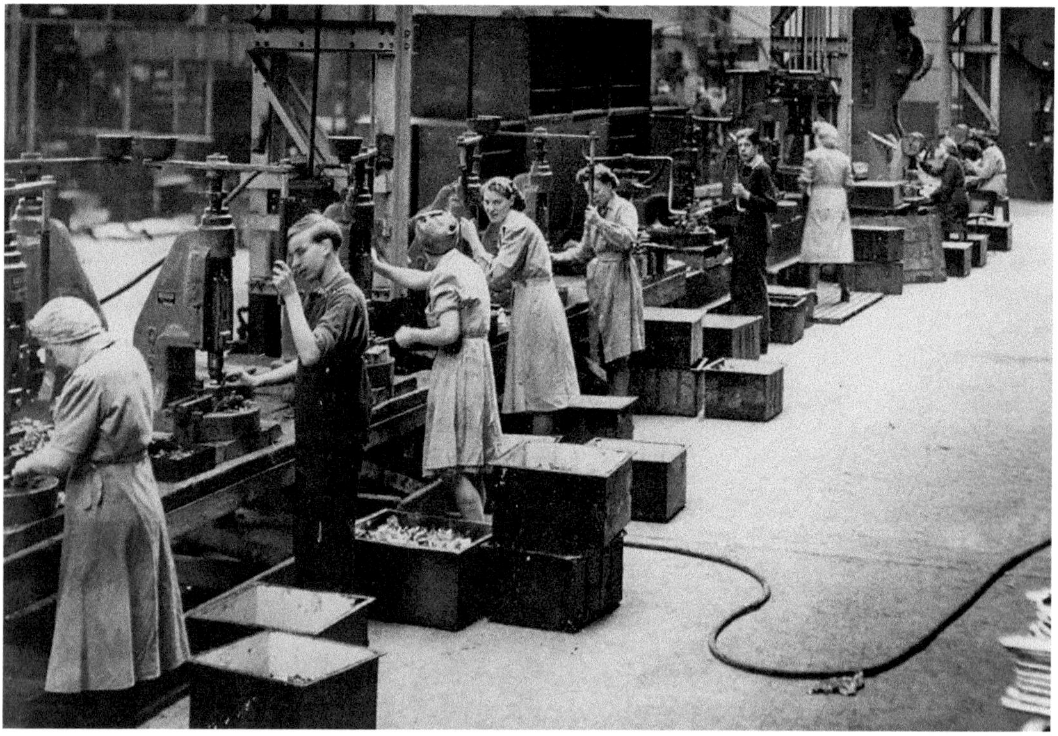

Female workers, Birtley Iron Co., 1945. (Photo courtesy of Gateshead Libraries)

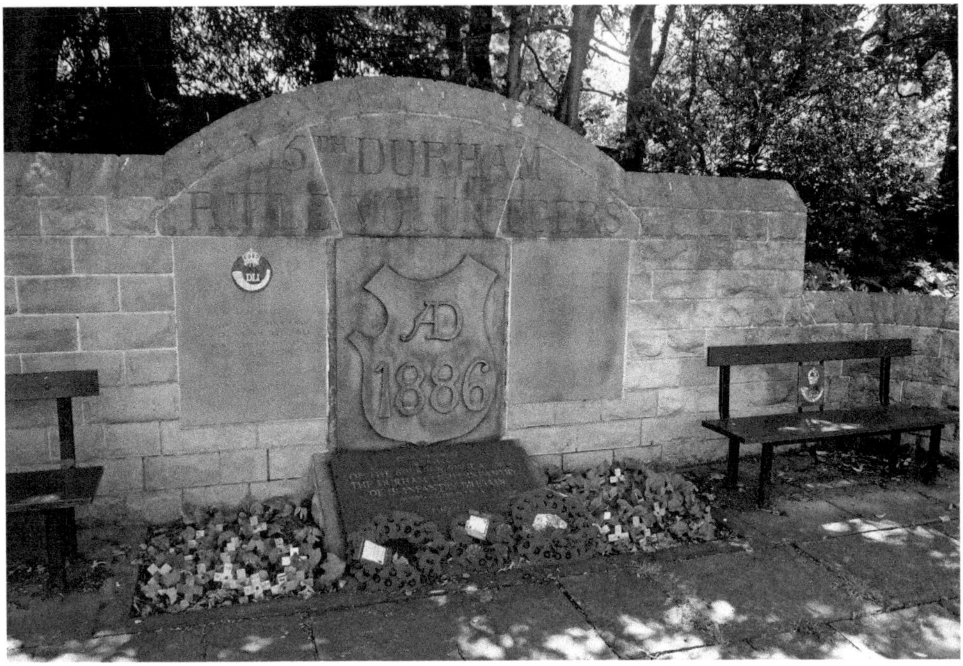

Durham Light Infantry war memorial in Saltwell Park.

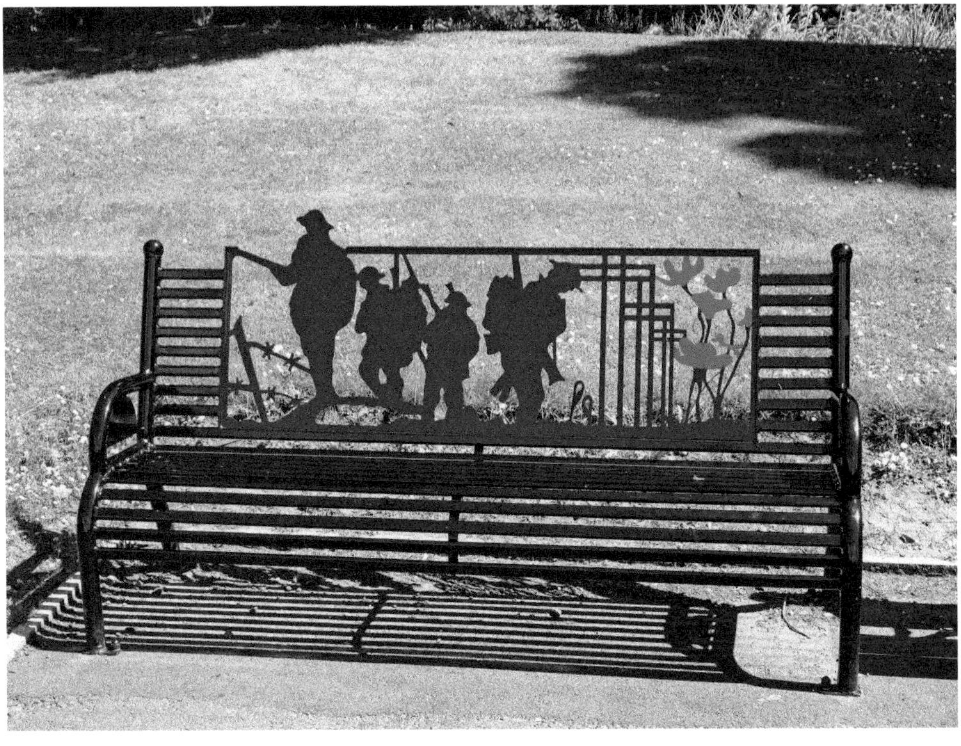

One of two memorial benches placed in Saltwell Park in 2015.

As Gateshead has grown, developed and changed over the decades, sadly it is inevitable that some war memorials may have to be relocated as buildings are demolished and new developments built in their place. That's what happened to a 2-tonne marble tablet that had been lost for fifty years and turned up in a council depot in 2006. It had previously been a First World War memorial stone from the former Park Terrace Presbyterian Church in Gateshead, and how it ended up spending fifty years in the lonely corner of a council depot is a mystery that will never likely be solved. The church was demolished in 1964 to make way for the St Cuthbert's village development, which itself has now been demolished.

One of the twenty-seven soldiers commemorated on the stone, Private George Wood, is listed as a member of the Royal Engineers. He was killed in action, aged twenty-six, near Armentieres in France in September 1915.

To pay their respects to one of their own, more than twenty Gateshead-based apprentices from the 103 (Tyne Electrical Engineers) Field Squadron Royal Engineers volunteered to help create a memorial garden in May 2017 with the newly erected memorial stone as the centrepiece.

The work was funded with the help of a grant of £9,600 from the Heritage Lottery Fund's First World War 'Then and Now' programme.

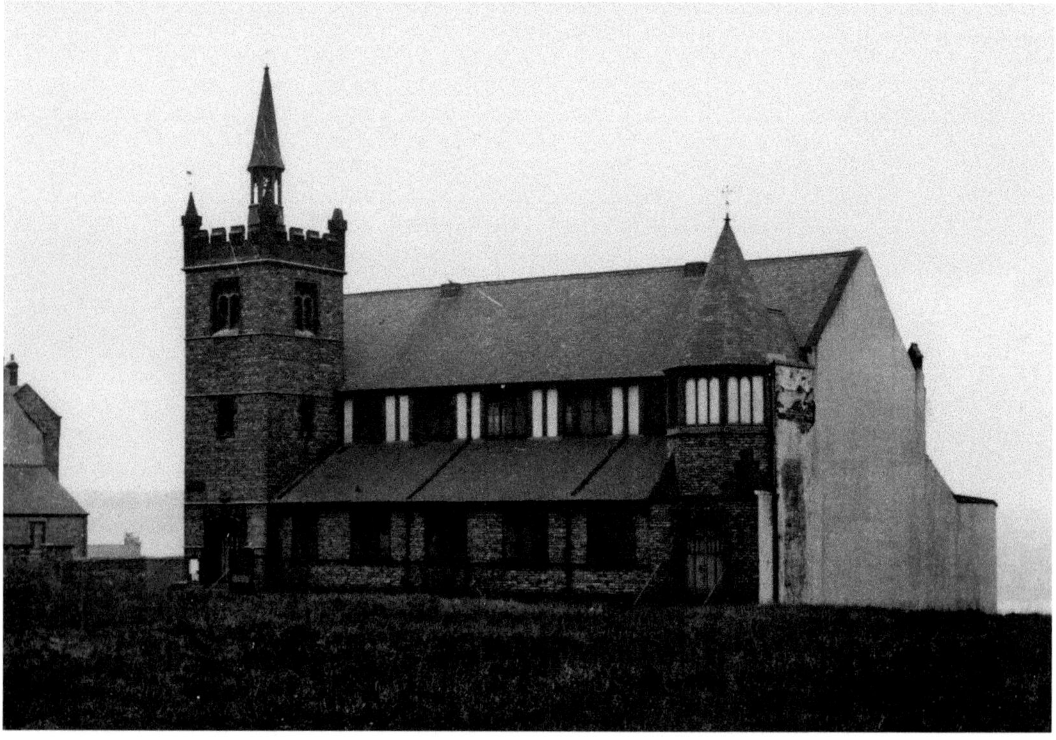

Presbyterian church where the memorial used to stand in 1963. (Photo courtesy of Gateshead Libraries)

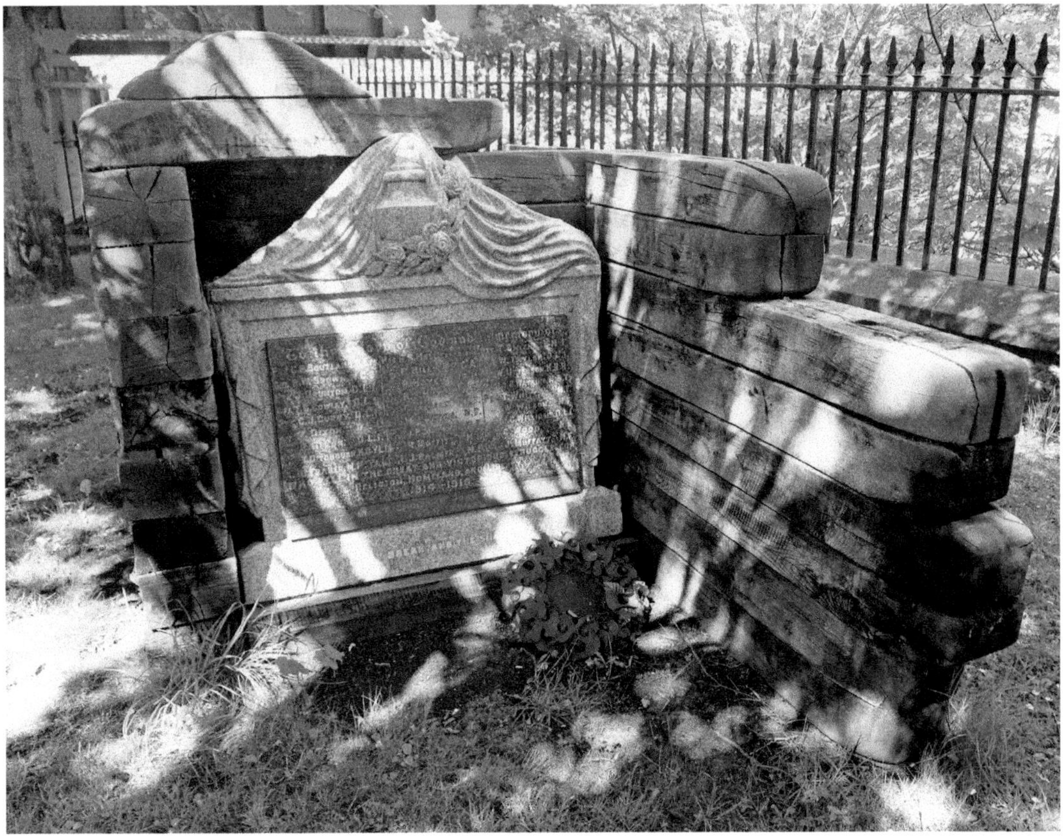

Newly erected First World War memorial at St Mary's Heritage Centre.

6. In TV and Film

Landmarks in the north-east have a history of appearing in television and film. Alnwick Castle appeared as Hogwarts in the Harry Potter films and, more recently, featured in the 2017 Hollywood blockbuster *Transformers: The Last Knight*, which was also filmed at Bamburgh and Newcastle city centre was brought to a standstill as a high-speed car chase was filmed. Roman Polanski's 1971 production of *Macbeth* was filmed in Northumberland and also made use of the dunes at Bamburgh, whereas the 2016 film *Lady Macbeth* was made in County Durham. We've also a wealth of TV shows filmed wholly, or partially, in the region including *Byker Grove* (the launch pad for Ant and Dec's phenomenal career, which was actually filmed in Benwell), the *Likely Lads, Whatever Happened to the Likely Lads, Vera, Spender, Our Friends in the North* and *Super Gran.* Newcastle-upon-Tyne, County Durham and Northumberland are well represented in both television and film, but what of Gateshead?

Mike Hodges' 1971 gangster movie *Get Carter*, starring Michael Caine in the title role, is the best-known portrayal of Gateshead. *Get Carter* is the gritty tale of London gangster Jack Carter, who comes to the north-east looking for his brother's killers and to extract his brutal revenge. Director Mike Hodges said he wanted to find a 'really hard place' to set the film and settled on Tyneside. The film was shot across Tyneside, but undoubtedly the most iconic location in the film was the Trinity Square multistorey car park in Gateshead. In one of the film's most famous scenes Jack Carter beats local businessman and small-time villain Cliff Brumby senseless and throws him from the top of the car park. The movie has acquired a cult following over the years, and led to Trinity Square multistorey being known as the 'Get Carter' car park.

DID YOU KNOW?

Gateshead Council sold off fragments of the Trinity Square car park remains as 'commemorative pieces of concrete in specially decorated tins' for £5 each.

The car park was confirmed for demolition in 2007, which led to an outcry for it to be preserved as a cinematic landmark, even Sylvester Stallone lent his weight to the argument – he had appeared in the 2000 remake of *Get Carter* (which substituted Gateshead for Las Vegas) – but the car park's fate was sealed, and in 2010 it was torn down.

It was replaced with a contemporary public square with a 27-foot-tall sculpture called *Halo.* It's home to one of the largest Tesco Extra stores in the country, a Vue cinema,

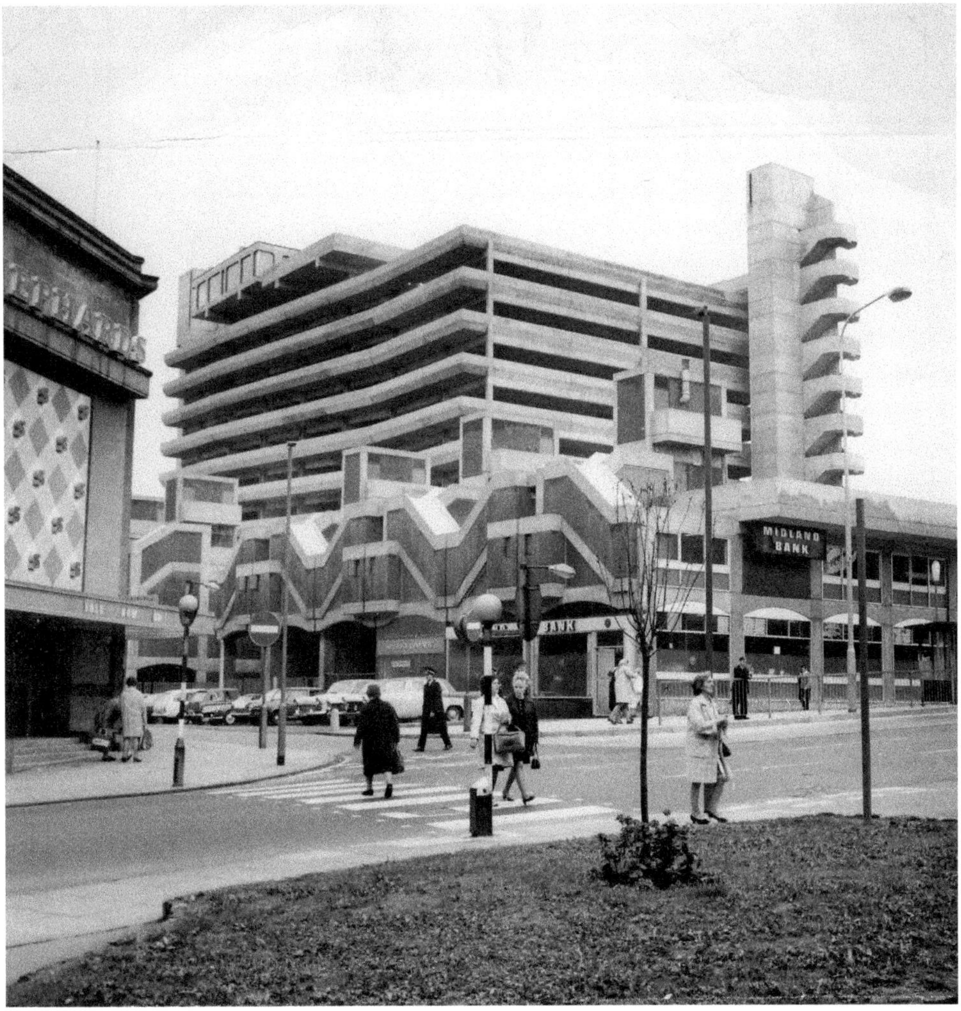

Get Carter car park. (Photo courtesy of Gateshead Libraries)

a Nandos, office space, accommodation for students, as well as a number of independent local shops and national retail stores.

Interestingly, *Get Carter* was preceded with another gritty crime drama back in 1961 that was filmed across the north-east. *Payroll* was one of the very first films to be shot predominantly in Newcastle and the surrounding area, and told the dark story of a gang of criminals who plan to roll a payroll van containing the wages of a local factory, with disastrous consequences.

The director, Sydney Hayers, told a local newspaper of his reasons for choosing the north-east as the setting for his movie: 'Provincial towns have much more to offer in atmosphere. Even there transport looks so different. Too often in the past people have been presented with shots of Big Ben, the Houses of Parliament, and the white cliffs of Dover to be told "This is England". It's not good enough.'

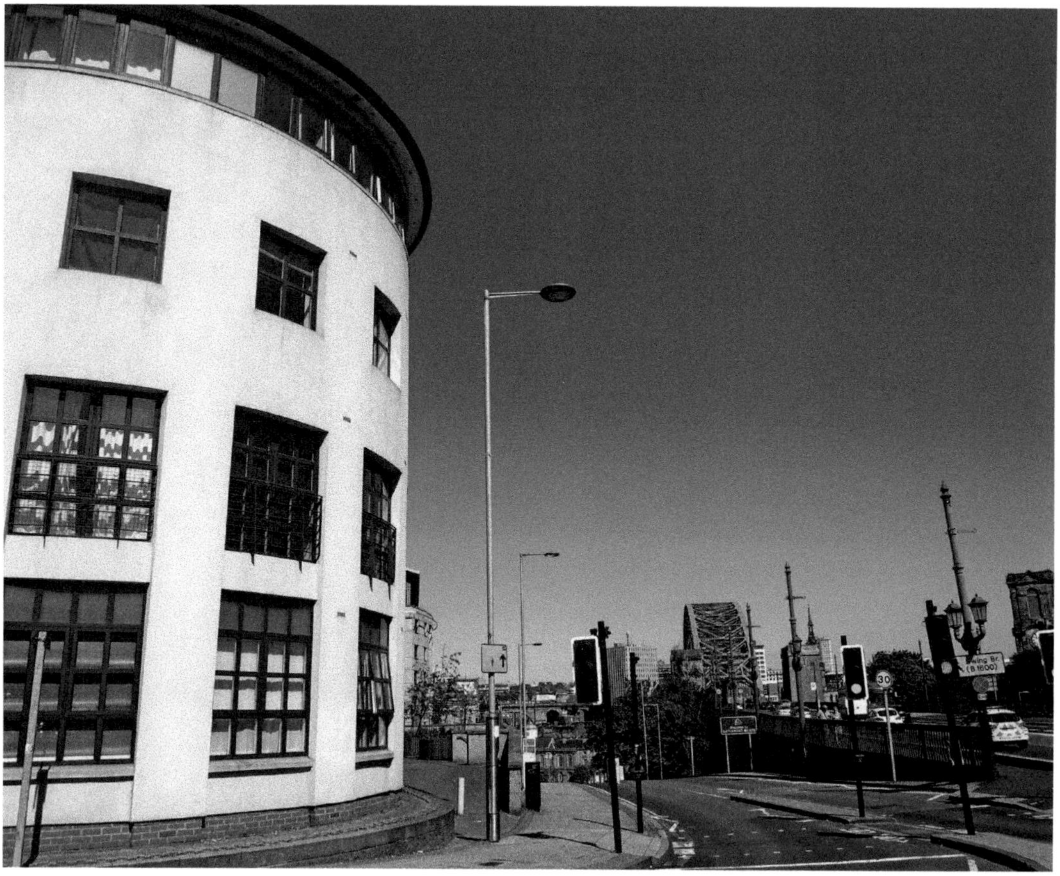

The building on Bottle Bank in the foreground stands on the site of the pub that appeared in *Payroll*.

Gateshead featured onscreen as the titular payroll van drove along Redheugh Road after crossing the junction of Askew Road. A character was thrown out of a pub on Bottle Bank, which has since been redeveloped to the extent that it is almost unrecognisable – save for the unmistakable Tyne Bridge in the shot.

Purely Belter was released in 2000 and the comedy drama tells the story of two teenage Newcastle United supporters trying to raise £1,000, by whatever means necessary, to buy two season tickets to their beloved football team. The film was shot entirely on Tyneside, with a number of landmarks in Newcastle featuring including Northumberland Street, Grey's Monument, the Central Arcade and St James' Park. Gateshead also appeared prominently on film, with scenes filmed at the Metrocentre, Dunston Staiths and the Angel of the North. Dunston Staiths is where the lads plan out their scams, and they see the Angel of the North as their very own 'guardian angel of toe-rags'.

Production Designer on the film, Don Taylor, said of the Angel of the North: 'The first time I stood underneath the Angel, I found it a strangely spiritual experience. Trying to film it, of course, was a far less heavenly affair, but the footage we have of it gives real power to the film.'

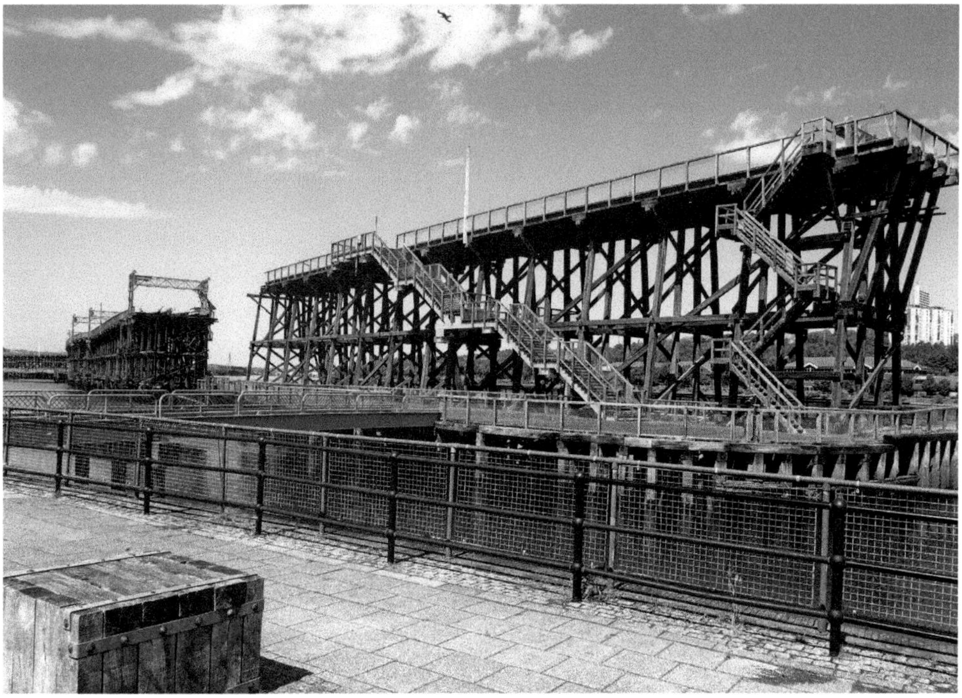

Durham Staiths, which featured in *Purely Belter*.

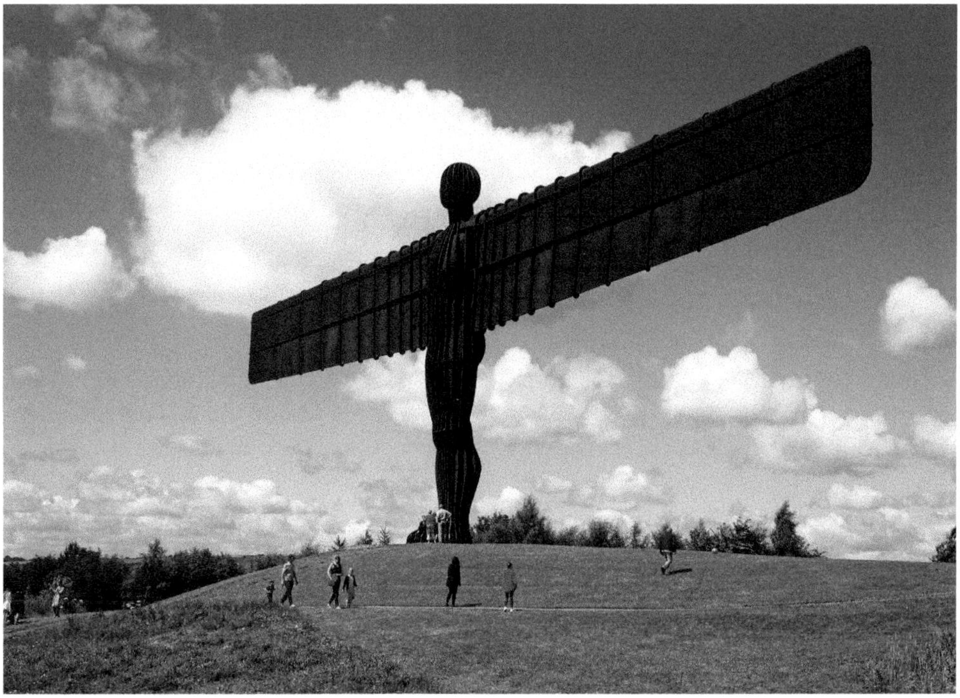

The Angel of the North.

DID YOU KNOW?

Sunderland AFC's Stadium of Light doubles, at times, in *Purely Belter* as St James' Park, the home of Newcastle United. Sacrilege!

Hollywood might have overlooked Gateshead, but Bollywood have come to town on no less than two occasions. The first occasion was in 2008 when a major Indian movie called *Hum Tum Aur Ghost* was entirely shot at landmarks across the region. The unofficial remake of the Ricky Gervais movie *Ghost Town* from the same year starred some of Bollywood's biggest stars and saw fans clambering for their autographs as they filmed across Newcastle and Gateshead during a three-month period over the summer, with locations south of the Tyne including the iconic Angel of the North. However, upon the movie's release in 2010, even the Angel couldn't save the movie from disappointing reviews, and its poor box office returns saw it given 'disaster' status by Box Office India.

DID YOU KNOW?

Hum Tum Aur Ghost translated is 'We You and Ghost'.

The year 2011 saw the release of *Phirr*, an Indian romantic thriller, filmed extensively in the north-east. The Angel of the North was chosen, once again, for inclusion; the Millennium Bridge featured too, as did Gateshead's Town Hall. Upon release *Phirr* fared a little better than *Hum Tum Aur Ghost*, being met with mixed reviews and a reasonable return at the box office.

The Angel of the North was once more the star of the silver screen, featuring in 2012's *The Liability* with Hollywood star Tim Roth – star of *Pulp Fiction*, *Reservoir Dogs* and *The Hateful Eight* – in the lead role. The thriller was shot at a range of other locations all over the north-east including Holy Island, Hexham and the Northumberland Coast.

Stormy Monday was a 1988 film starring a young Sean Bean in the role of Brendan, a janitor at a Newcastle nightclub. A host of other big names starred, including Tommy Lee Jones, Melanie Griffith and Geordie megastar Sting. The film features landmarks across Newcastle and Gateshead, including the Metrocentre (which had only opened two years earlier) and the Tyne Bridge, and the High Level Bridge played host to an important meeting between the rival nightclub owners played by Tommy Lee Jones and Sting.

Melanie Griffith, who rented a house in Darras Hall, near Ponteland, during the filming of the movie said at the time: 'It's just so pretty and the people are so great,' she said. 'I am seriously considering buying a place here ... I have done a little sight-seeing and I want to drive to Durham to see the wonderful cathedral.' She added: 'Newcastle is a wonderful city with all the old buildings. We just don't have them in America.'

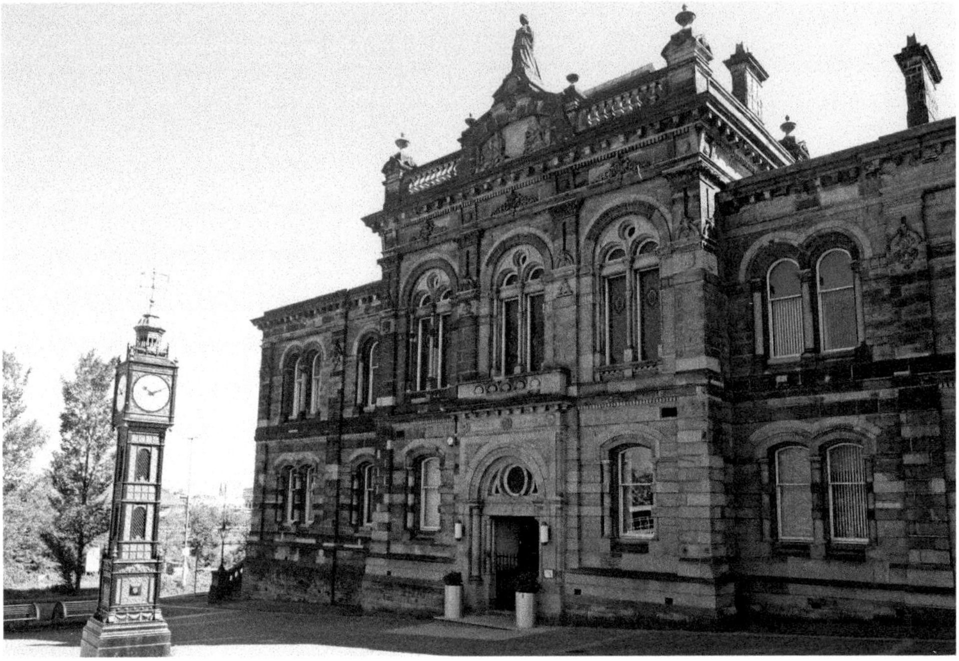

The Town Hall as seen in *Phirr*.

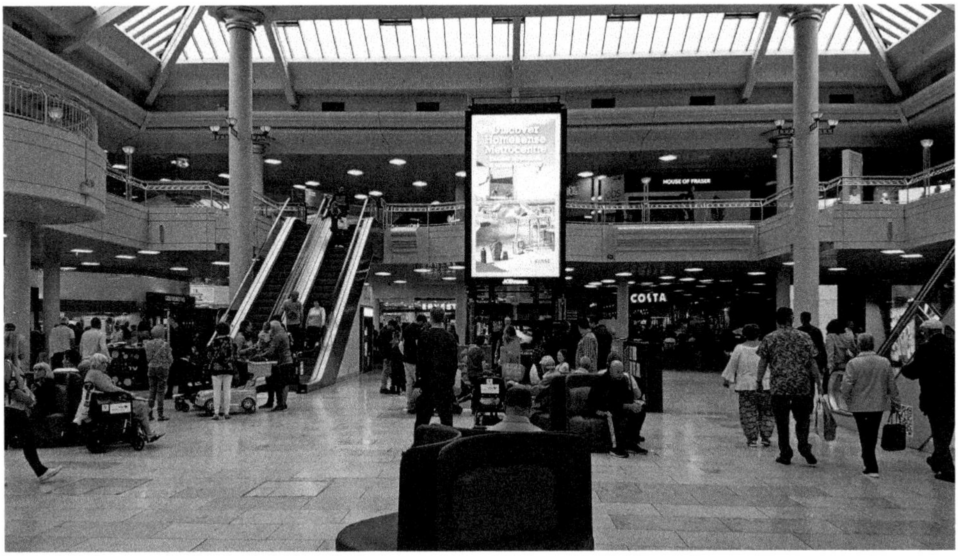

The intu Metrocentre.

Despite the rich tapestry of television programmes set in the north-east, Gateshead isn't represented quite as well as its neighbour across the Tyne, but that's not to say that it's been completely overlooked.

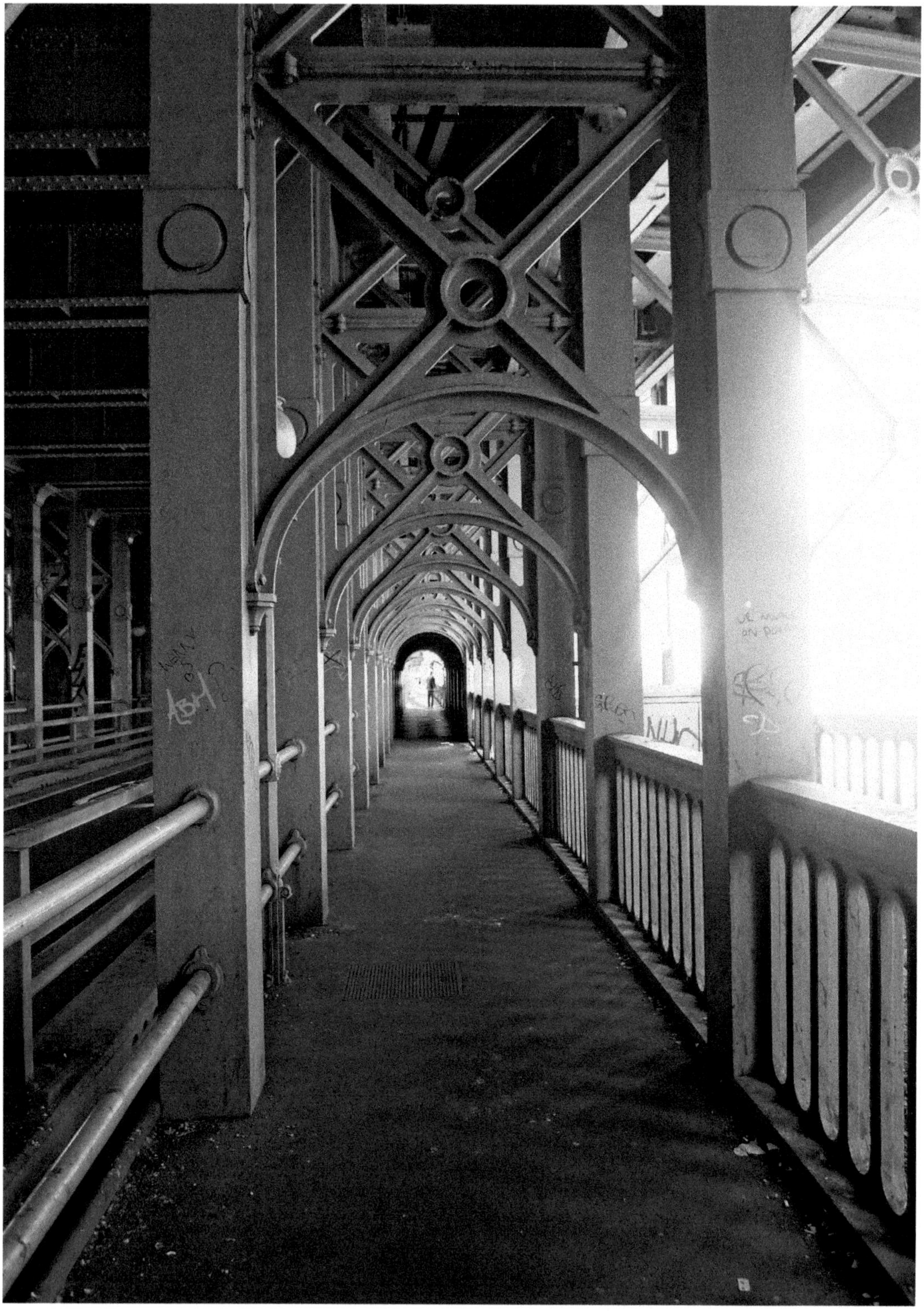

The High Level Bridge, the location of a key scene in *Stormy Monday*.

One of the best-loved television shows all of time is *Auf Wiedersehen Pet*, the comedy drama which, in 1983, saw three Geordie bricklayers – Dennis, played by Tim Healy; Neville, played by Kevin Whatley; and Oz, played by Jimmy Nail – head to Germany in search of work that didn't exist back home in 'Thatcher's Britain'. There they shared a hut on a building site and forged a friendship and bond, with Barry played by Timothy Spall, Bomber played by Pat Roach, Wayne played by Gary Holton and Moxey played by Christopher Fairbank. Gateshead is mentioned in the very first episode, when Oz, after visiting Germany's biggest brothel famously exclaims: 'I'll tell you one thing mate, sex is in its infancy in Gateshead!'

During series 1 and 2, Oz's flat back home is in Gateshead and, despite there being a number of scenes back in the north-east, Gateshead itself only makes one solitary appearance across all four series and the special. It is at very beginning of series 3 during the opening credits: we see a Native American sitting cross-legged on an Indian reservation chanting, and when he looks up it cuts to the Angel of the North.

Interestingly, Gateshead forms part of the dialogue in series 2. It's very telling in how Gateshead was perceived when the series was aired in 1986. Barry arrives unexpectedly at Neville's house in Newcastle and when asked where he's been, he says: 'Some place they call Gateshead, talk about the bleeding concrete jungle.'

Going back even further, there was a children's series in the late 1970s about the adventures of J. G., Ian, Gog, Baz and Sam, who delivered newspapers to the people of the north-east for local newsagent Jack Crawford, played by Glynn Edwards. *The Paper Lads* was first broadcast on 24 August 1977 and ran for two series of seven episodes each, until January 1979.

This largely forgotten programme was described by Tyne Tees as 'a nice, lively blend of excitement, drama and humour and definitely for all ages.' One of the writers, William Corlett, won a Best Childrens's Television Writer of the Year award for the four episodes of the show he contributed.

The show was made on location in Tyneside, mostly across Gateshead with terraced streets in the Bensham and Teams areas. Sadly, the majority of the streets that featured have since been bulldozed to make way for more modern housing. The paper shop itself has also been pulled down – an area of grass is all that remains.

Now let's take a look at a much more recent children's TV programme made in Gateshead. In September 2012, *Wolfblood*, a new fantasy drama for children, first appeared on CBBC. It starred a Geordie teenager in the lead role playing Maddy, who appears normal during the day but is secretly part of an ancient race called Wolfbloods, which means that she transformers into a wolf with incredible powers after dark. Gateshead provides the backdrop for the multiple award-winning show, which has recently seen its fifth series aired. The Charles Thorp Comprehensive School on Hookergate Campus doubles for the fictional Bradlington High School, and the woodland around Rowland Gill countryside featured heavily for the after dark scenes.

Prior to the first series appearing on TV, Aimee Kelly, who appears in the lead role, and grew up in Fenham, told newspapers: 'We filmed in and around Rowlands Gill and Blanchland. The field and woods would get quite creepy at night with our fake smoke.' From series 4 filming moved to Heworth Grange Comprehensive and areas within Windy Nook and Newcastle.

In 2013 a documentary hit our screens based around the national bakery chain Greggs, which started in 1951 here in the north-east. *More than Meats the Pie* provided viewers

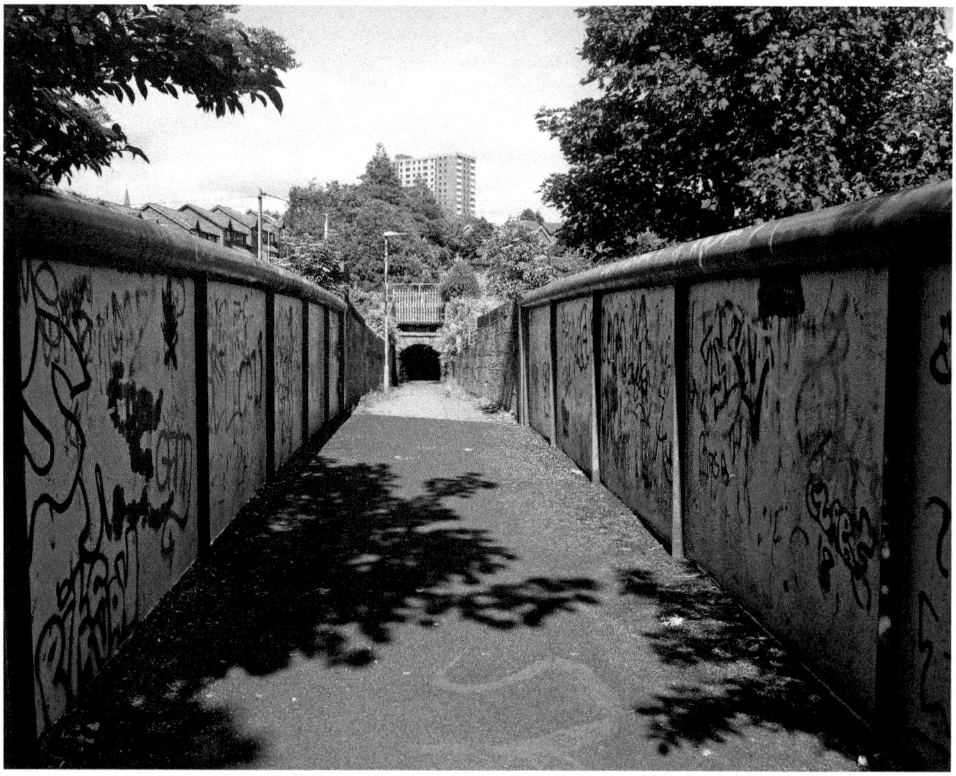

The footbridge in Bensham over the East Coast Railway, seen in the opening credits of *The Paper Lads* as Andrew Edwards, as Ian, crosses.

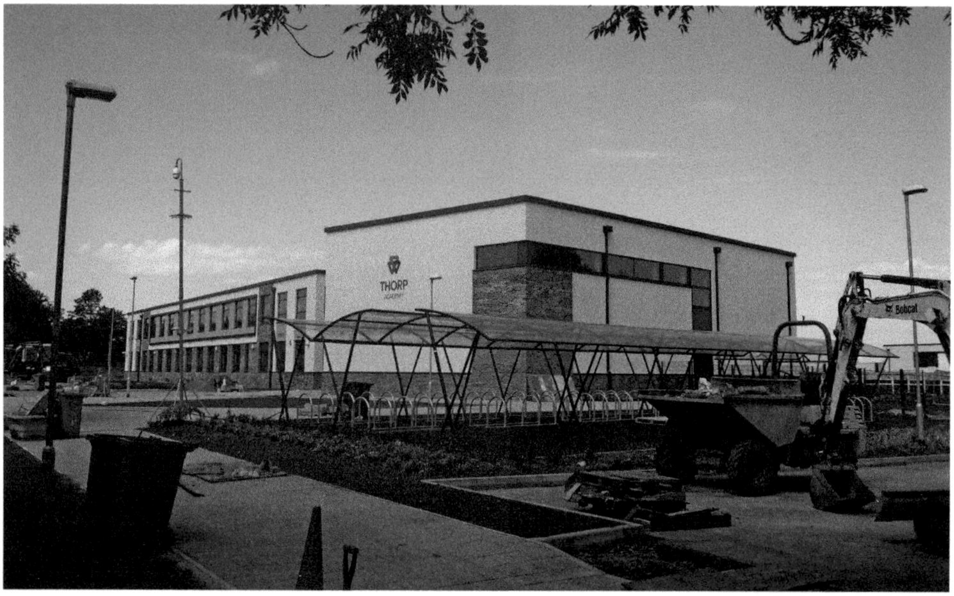

Charles Thorp Comprehensive School, in the midst of a redevelopment programme.

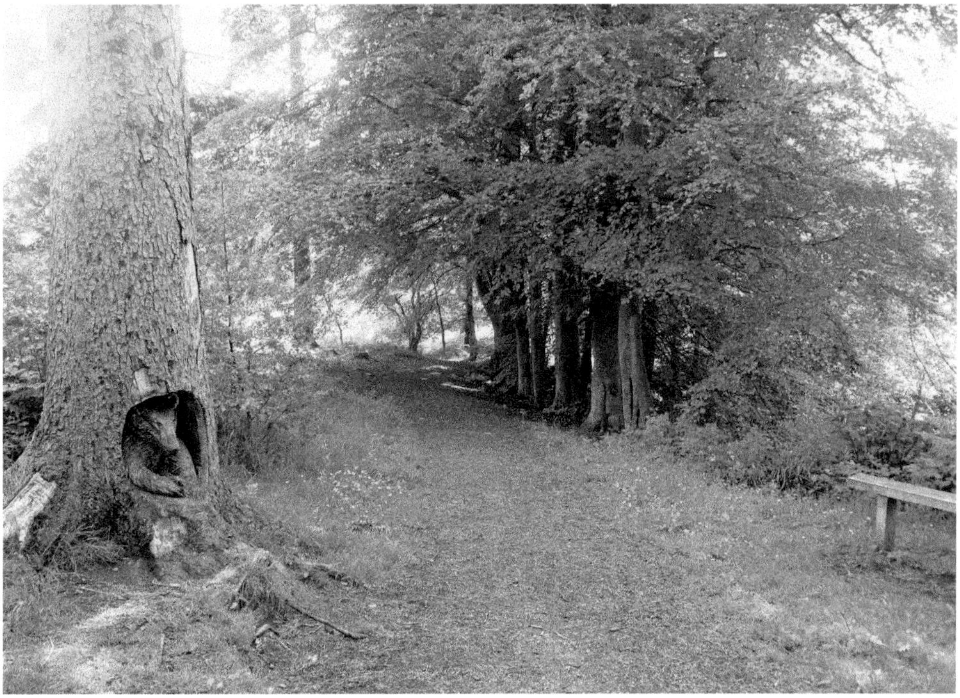

The Rowlands Gill countryside.

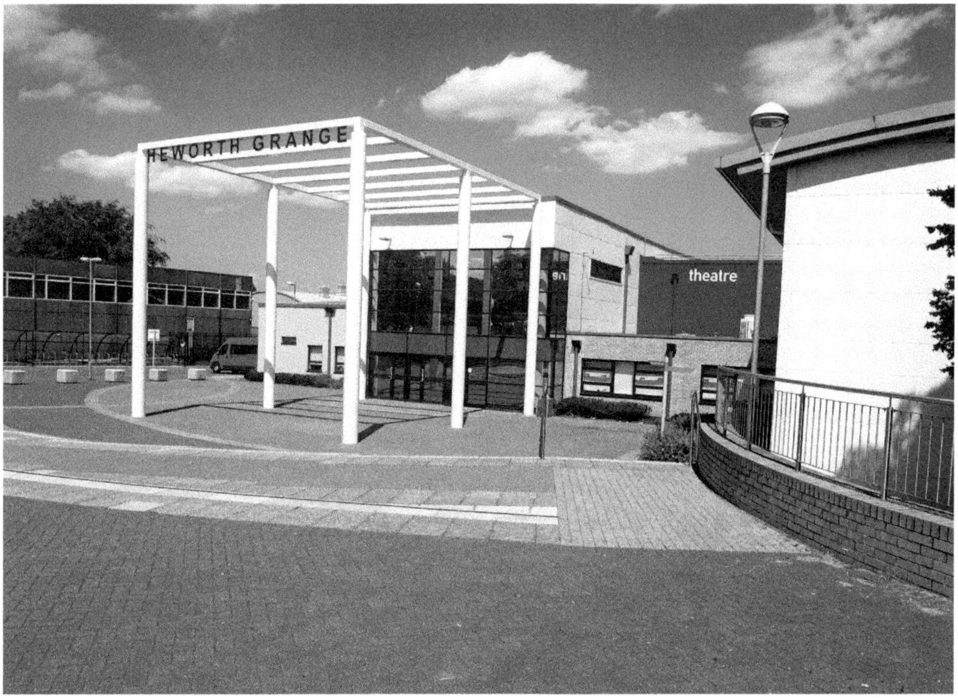

Heworth Grange Comprehensive School.

with a glimpse behind the counters and in the kitchens and factories, which focussed on the north-east stores including Gosforth Park, Northumberland Street in Newcastle, Low Fell and Gateshead town centre.

In 2014, the *X Factor,* arguably the biggest event annual event in television, saw the Sage in Gateshead used as the venue for the north-east auditions. Fans and hopefuls queued for hours, with many hoping to get a glimpse of the judges and one in particular being a favourite among the crowd: the north-east's very own Cheryl Cole. The auditions returned to Gateshead in 2017.

Back in 2010 the streets of Gateshead were chosen to be the backdrop for a new Hovis advert set in the 1970s. The production company Gorgeous Enterprises said they chose Tyneside locations because they 'looked like the 70s'. Ian Mearns, Gateshead MP, leapt to the defence of the town: 'If they looked hard enough in any town throughout the whole of the country they would find locations of that age. I guess they chose Gateshead because they found a lot of locations from that age very close together.' He added that while Gateshead does have some rundown buildings, it also has modern architecture such as the Sage. Vehicles from the decade were brought in for filming, with vintage cars, buses and bicycles giving the advert an authentic 1970s feel.

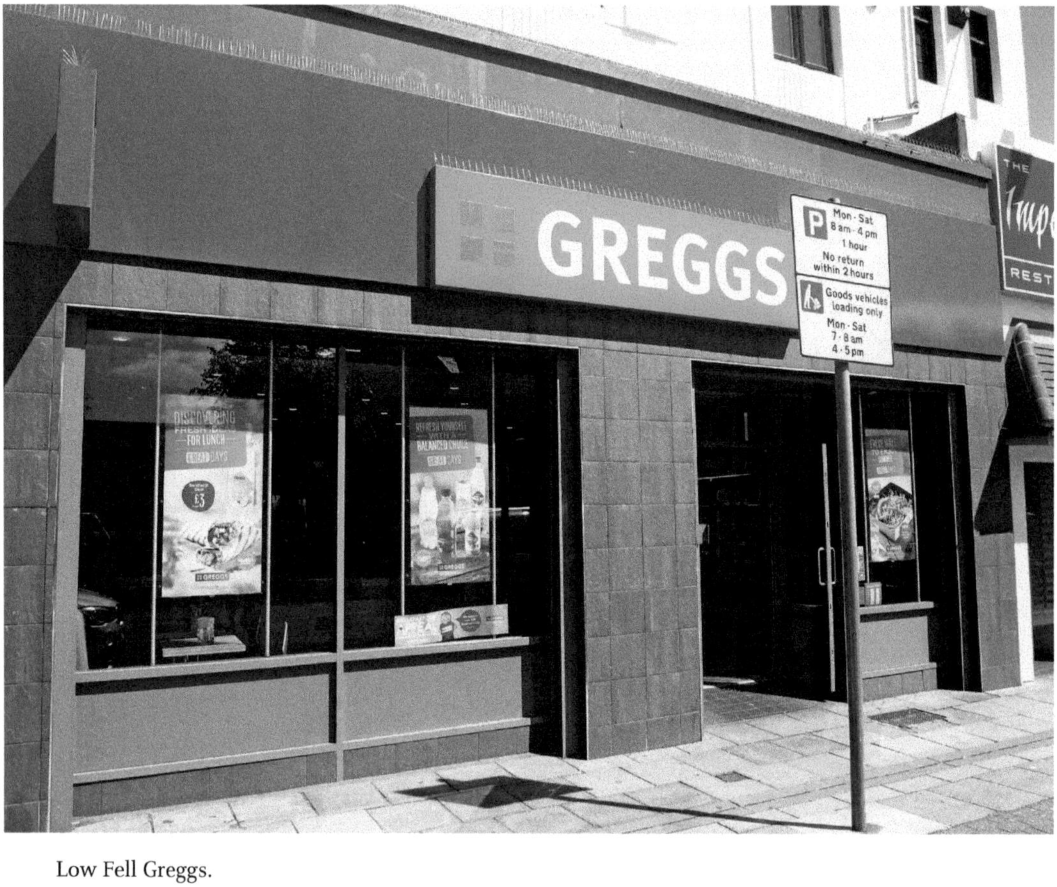

Low Fell Greggs.

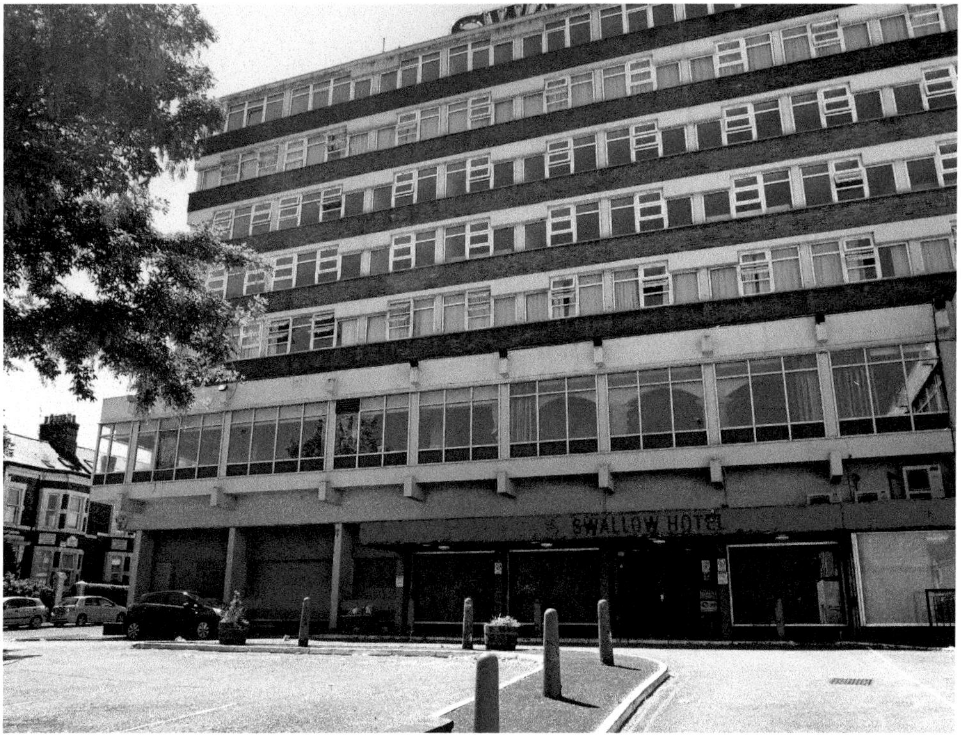

Swallow Hotel, which sadly closed down in 2014 and is now being converted into a Jewish residential college.

Filming began at the Swallow Hotel in High West Street, Gateshead, with locals being given the chance to appear as extras complete with 1970s fashion including flares and flat caps.

Launderama, a laundrette on Whitehall Road, was chosen for one of the scenes thanks to its dated interior.

Paul Wood, owner of Launderama, said: 'Gorgeous Enterprises expressed an interest in filming here and came and had a look round a few times. The shop is very much unchanged and it's an old design. 'They are actually painting it a different colour and changing the panels on the front of the machines to look like they're from the 70s.'

Back in the 1970s there was an advert made for Tudor Crisps, a brand of potato crisps manufactured in Sandyford in Newcastle. The advert saw a Geordie paper lad picking up his papers and taking a few bags of Tudor out of his wages. He then bribed another young lad saying he'll give him a 'canny bag of crisps'. The lad responds 'Whey aye man, they're Tudor, I'll climb a mountain', then realises that he's going to have to do just that, as he looks up at a huge tower block of flats.

The tower block was the Derwent Tower in Dunston. The twenty-nine storey tower block was designed by the Owen Luder Partnership who had previously designed the *Get Carter* car park. During its construction, which began in 1968, locals nicknamed it the Dunston Rocket due to its unusual shape. The nickname stuck throughout its life until it was demolished in 2012.

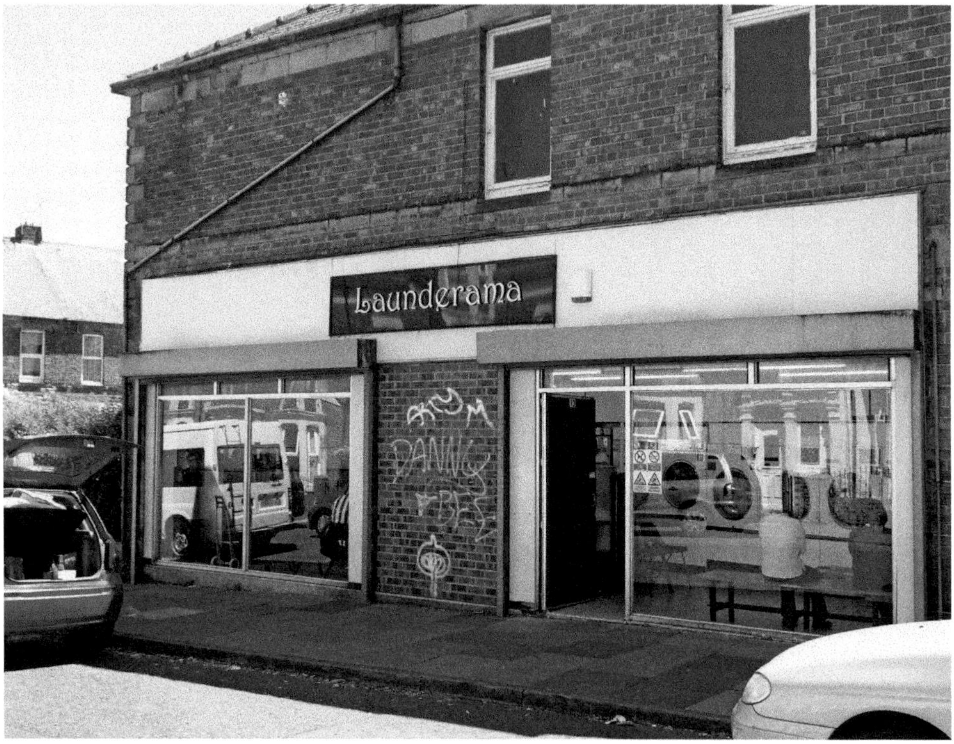

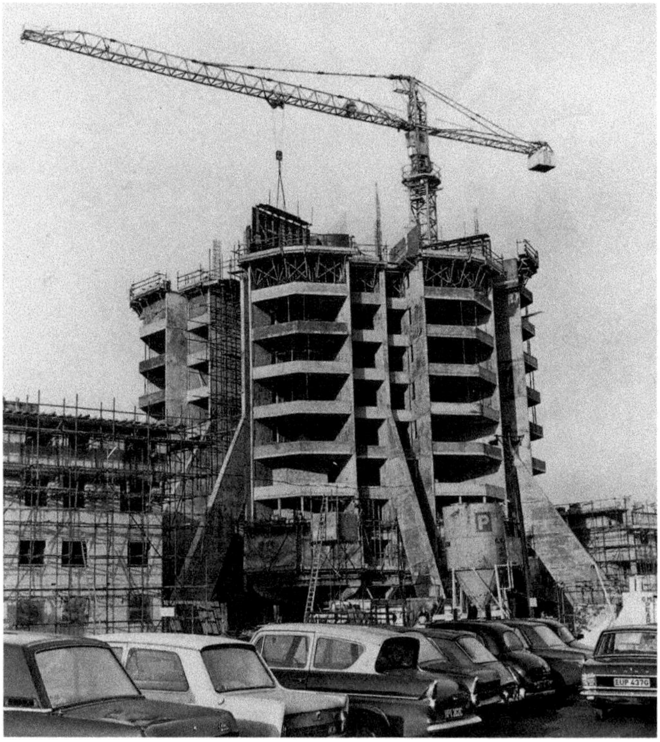

Above: Launderama.

Left: The Dunston Rocket being constructed in 1969. (Photo courtesy of Gateshead Libraries)

7. Into the Twenty-First Century

The novelist and playwright J. B. Priestley wrote of Gateshead in his bestselling 1934 travelogue *English Journey*:

> If there is any town of like size on the continent of Europe than can show a similar lack of civic dignity and all the evidence of urban civilization, I should like to know its name and quality. No true civilization could have produced such a town, which is nothing better than a huge dingy dormitory ... The whole town appeared to have been carefully planned by an enemy of the human race. Insects can do better than this.

Gateshead today bears little resemblance to the Gateshead that J. B. Priestley wrote of when he penned his damning verdict of the town, which was filled with the sights and smells of a chemical works, flour mills, coal staiths, roperies and even a fat-rendering

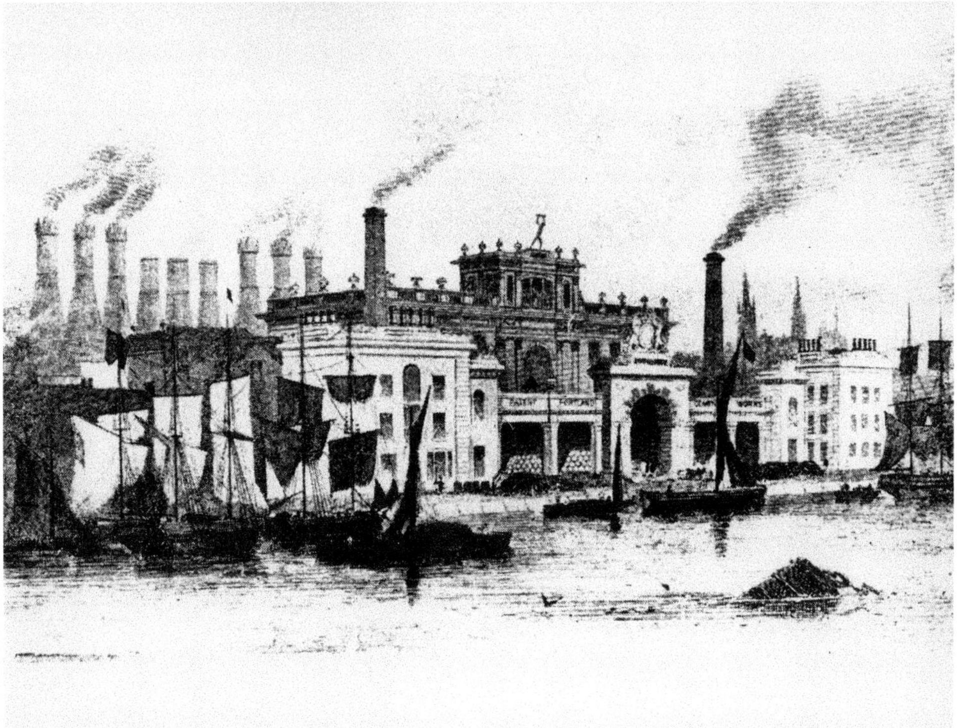

Engraving of Gateshead cement works on South Shore Road around 1850. (Photo courtesy of Gateshead Libraries)

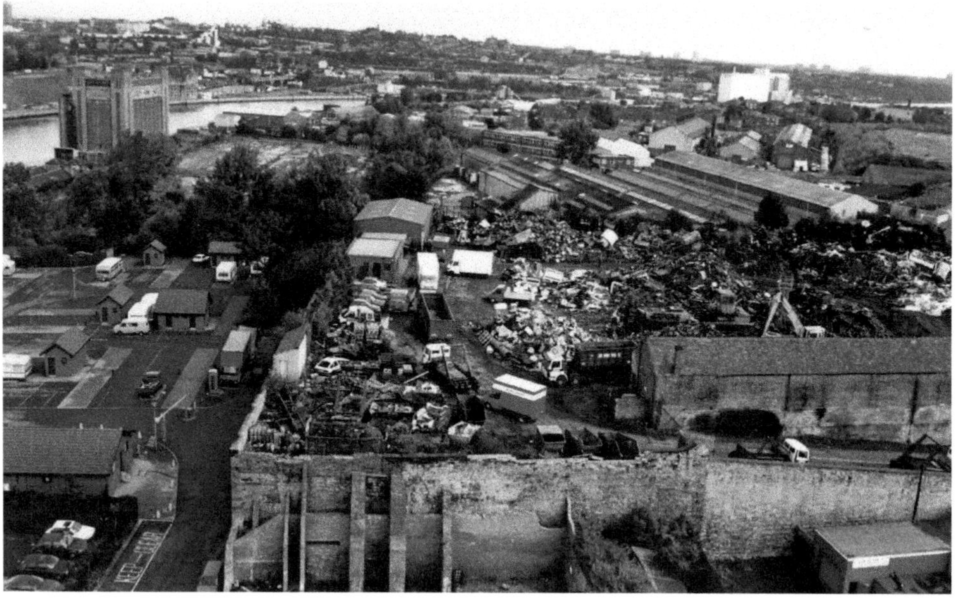

Jennings Scrap Yard in 1997, showing just how recently there was industry on Gateshead Quays. (Photo courtesy of Gateshead Libraries)

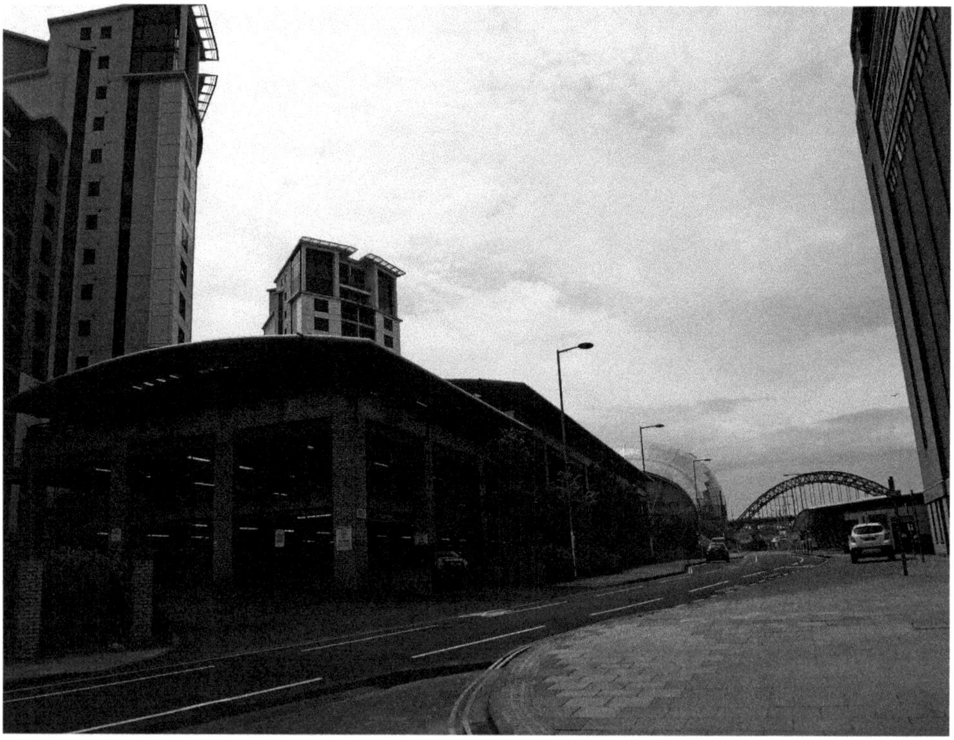

South Shore Road with the BALTIC Centre for Contemporary Art to the left and the Sage Gateshead ahead.

plant that lined the south side of the River Tyne. The town has been transformed in the decades since then, to the extent that in June 2011, when Google ran a competition to find Britain's best streets, over 20,000 votes were cast for South Shore Road on Gateshead's Quays, which was named 'Britain's Hippest Street'.

This award is testament to the work Gateshead Council has begun to develop the town, with a view to achieving city status. City status was applied for in 2012 as part of the Queen's Jubilee celebrations, but the bid failed. Council Leader Mick Henry said at the time:

> Naturally we're disappointed not to have been successful this time around, but we know we put together a good bid, which reflected the views of local people, and we gave it our all. The very process of bidding for city status has actually brought us benefits. It has highlighted just how positive, ambitious and forward thinking Gateshead is on a global stage. The fact that many people, here and abroad, already regard Gateshead as a city speaks volumes.

The most notable transformation so far has occurred on the Quays, with the Millennium Bridge, the Sage Gateshead and the Baltic Centre for Contemporary Art all being constructed since we entered the millennium. They combine to make the Gateshead Quay a truly awesome sight, but work has taken place right across the town, so let's explore some of the improvements that have occurred to bring Gateshead into the twenty-first century.

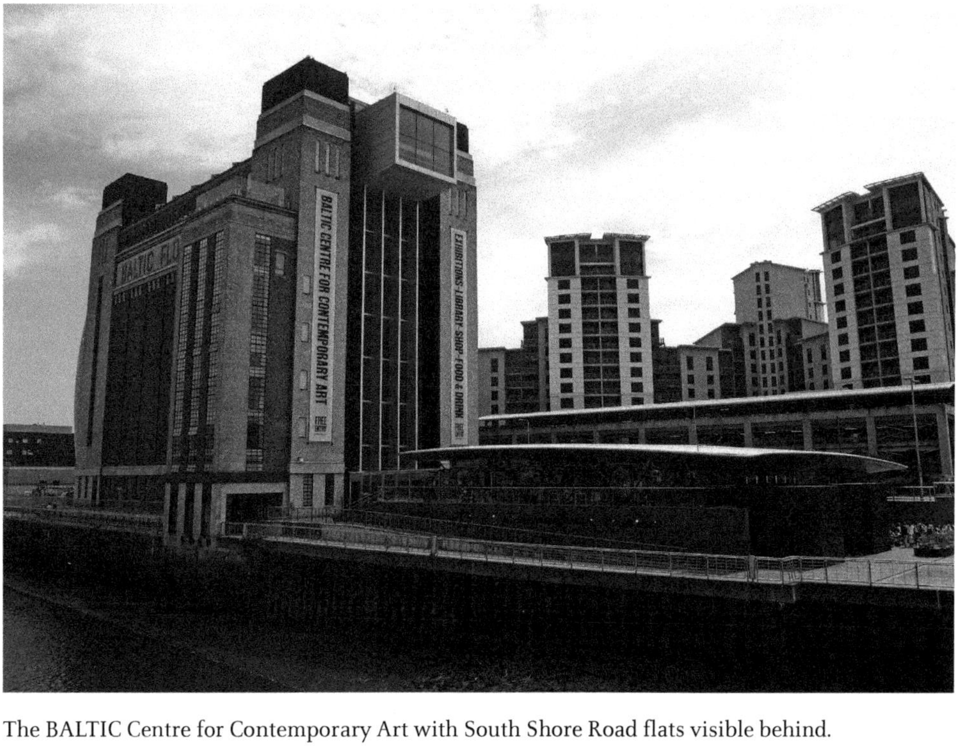

The BALTIC Centre for Contemporary Art with South Shore Road flats visible behind.

The Angel of the North, made of 200 tonnes of steel and standing 65 feet high with a 175-foot wingspan, dominates the skyline for miles around. Upon its conception, the Angel of the North generated much controversy in the media, with the British press running many negative news articles. Local councillors and public figures were also very vocal in their opposition to the sculpture. The official unveiling of the Angel occurred on 20 June 1998 and Gateshead Council hosted 'Celebrating an Angel' day – a free event including entertainment by musicians and artists, an opportunity to see Angel artwork by local children, and an auction of the No. 9 Newcastle United football shirt in which the Angel had been draped amid much publicity. There was even the chance to meet the man behind the design of the angel: Antony Gormley.

Today the Angel of the North, despite its lonely position on a hilltop overlooking the A1 on the southern edge of Low Fell, is visited by over 150,000 people each year, and is seen by more than 90,000 drivers each day passing on the A1.

Despite the original opposition, the Angel has become a local landmark. It is often used to represent Tyneside – as it the Tyne Bridge and the Millennium Bridge – and almost twenty years on, the people of Gateshead are proud of 'their' Angel of the North.

The MetroCentre opened in two phases: the Red Mall opened on 28 April 1986, but the official opening was on 14 October 1986. The MetroCentre, the original mega mall, the

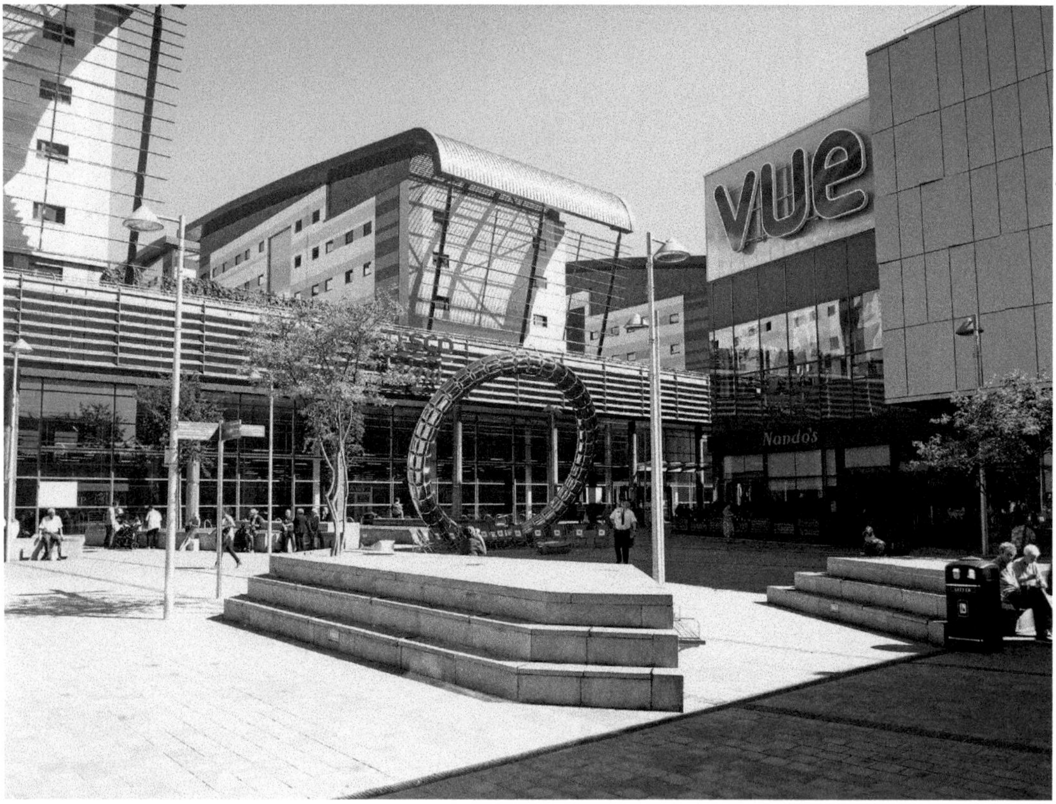

Trinity Square.

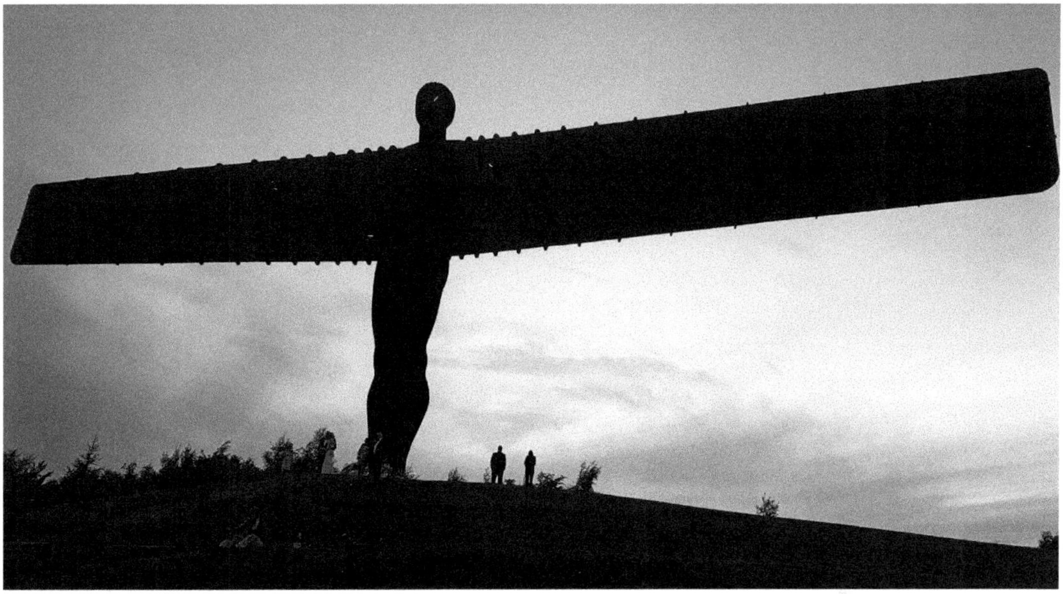

The Angel of the North at dusk.

size of which had never been seen before, opened to great excitement and curiosity. It was built on land purchased in the early 1970s for just £100,000 by property developer, and later Newcastle United owner, Sir John Hall.

In 1988 MetroLand opened at a cost of £20 million in the Yellow Mall, Europe's largest indoor amusement park including a roller coaster, pirate ship and Ferris wheel. MetroLand closed in 2008, despite strong local opposition and a petition with 4,000 signatures. The closure made way for a redevelopment and modernisation of the Yellow Mall, which now includes a new Odeon Cinema with an IMAX screen.

Today the recently rebranded intu Metrocentre has undertaken countless changes and improvements since it opened almost thirty years ago. Over half a billion shoppers have visited Europe's largest shopping centre since it first opened its doors and it now boasts over 340 stores populating the 1.9 million square feet of shopping and leisure space. Over 10,000 free car parking spaces and excellent transport links contribute to over 2.5 million visitors to the Metrocentre each year.

Saltwell Park was created on the 37-acre Saltwellside Estate that Gateshead Council purchased in 1875 for £35,000 from William Wailes, a leading exponent of stained glass who lived in the grand Victorian mansion called Saltwell Towers in the centre of the estate. The council rented Saltwell Towers back to Wailes for the remainder of his life.

The park was planned out by landscape designer Edward Kemp and became known informally as 'The People's Park', a nickname that is commonly used to this day. There was no officially opening ceremony but the park was used by the people of Gateshead from late 1876. Saltwell Park and the surrounding area have changed hugely since the park first opened for the people of the town. By the end of the twentieth century the park had been

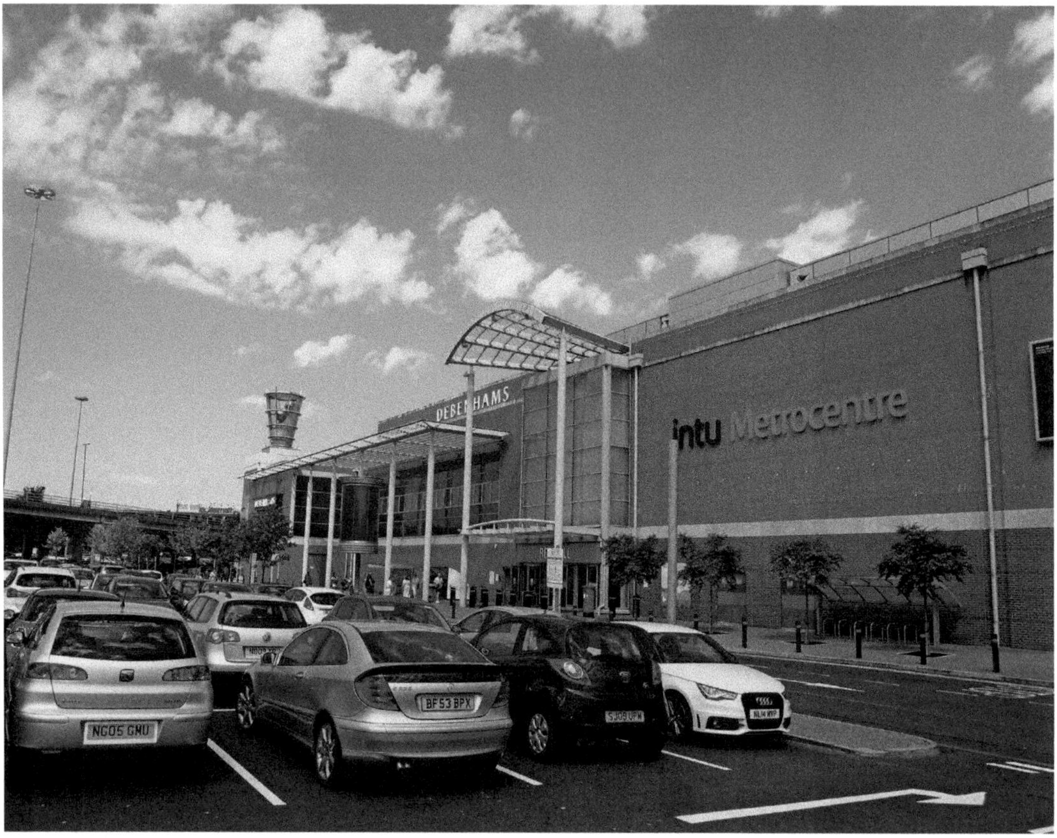

The intu Metrocentre.

neglected and fallen into disrepair. However between 1999 and 2005 a restoration project costing £9.6 million returned the park and Saltwell Tower to its Victorian splendour.

Saltwell Park is now visited by over 2 million people each year. In 2005 Saltwell Park was named 'Britain's Best Park', and the following year was chosen as the Civic Trust Park of the Year. Every year since 2006 it's won a Green Flag award, and in 2013 it was relisted as one of fifty-five Green Heritage sites in the UK. On Wednesday 14 July 2004 Saltwell Towers was reopened, having been converted into the visitor centre for the park, including a café, IT facilities and an exhibition on the fascinating history of the Saltwell Park and Towers.

DID YOU KNOW?

In Whitehead's Newcastle Directory for the years 1782–84, which were the first in which Gateshead was included, there were 145 listed tradesmen, and no less than sixty-five of those were situated in Bottle Bank on the Gateshead side of the river.

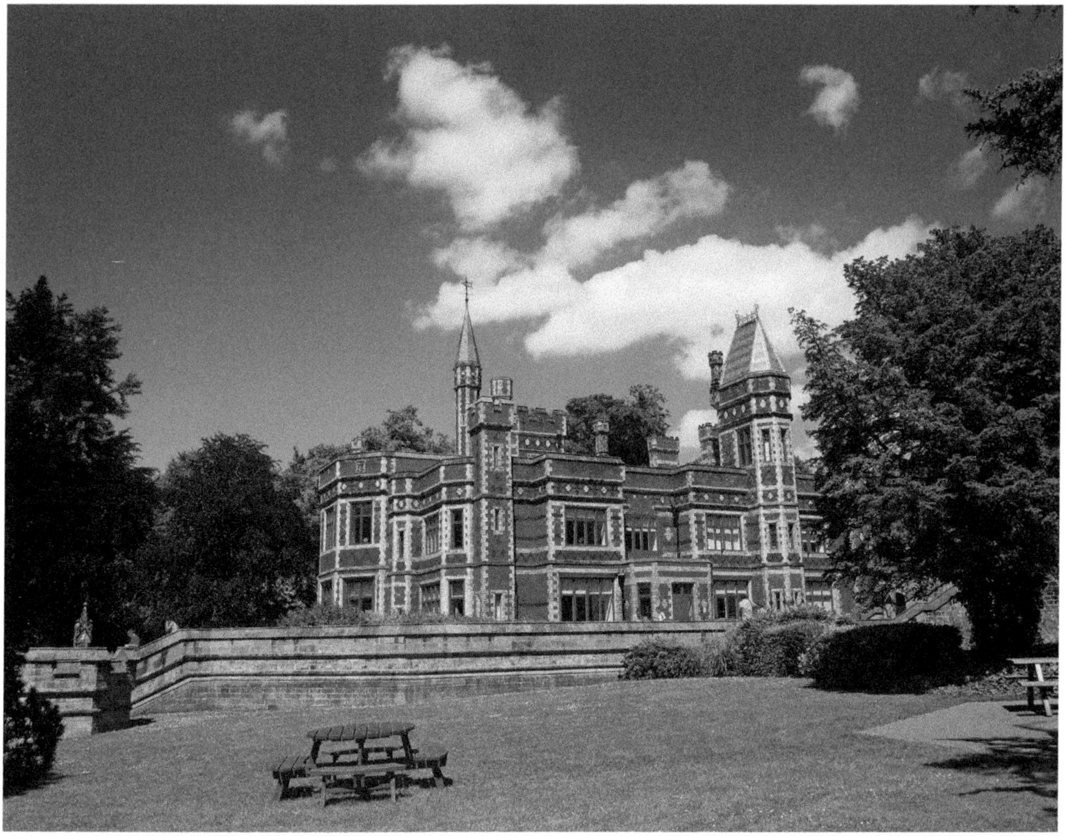

Saltwell Towers.

In 2005, the Society of Chief Architects of Local Authorities (SCALA) awarded the restored Saltwell Towers its Civic Building of the Year.

When Gateshead Town Hall opened in February 1870, this was the third building in Gateshead to have been designated town hall. The foundation stone had been laid two years earlier on 11 June 1868 by Mayor Robert Stirling Newall at a disastrous ceremony. Thousands of the town's residents turned up for the event and two special spectator platforms had been erected to accommodate the sizable crowd; however one of these platforms collapsed under the weight of 500 onlookers, and Mr Barnett, a seventy-year-old man from Windmill Hills, lost his life.

From that day forth many superstitious Gateshead residents feared the building may be cursed, and sadly more tragedy would befall the beautiful building in the years that followed. In 1935, Mayor Catherine White collapsed and died on the steps of the town hall. In 1950, a lady lost her foot in a frenzied scramble for tickets to that year's World Cup.

The town hall remained the centre of the town's government for over 100 years until the current Civic Centre opened in 1987. For decades the old building was used by the council for storage. This was until work began to refurbish the interior and exterior and bring the building back to its original grandeur. Sage Gateshead, five minutes away on

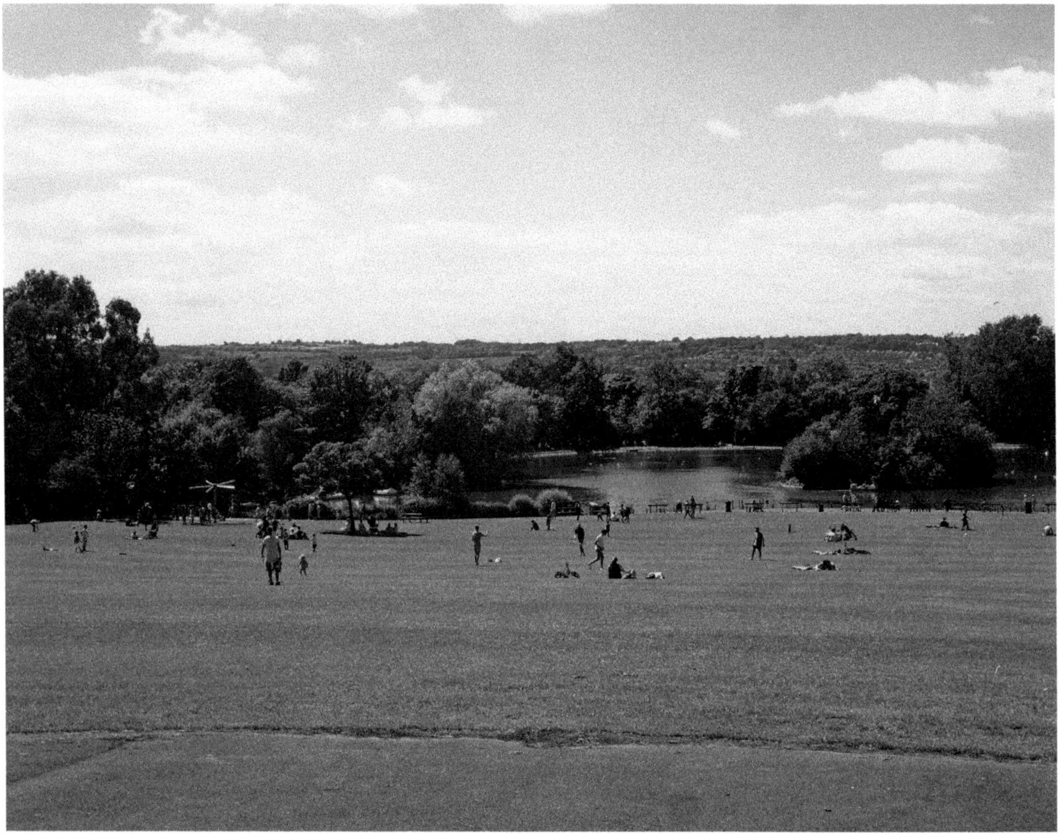

Saltwell Park on a summer's day.

the Quays, took over the management of the Grade II-listed building at the suggestion of Gateshead Council. In January 2014 the Old Town Hall was opened as an intimate venue for performance and the arts, as well as being a stunning location in which to host conferences, events and weddings.

St Mary's Church, a riverside landmark high above the River Tyne, was the only Anglican church in the town until St John's was built in 1825 at Sheriff Hill. This led to it being considered the 'mother church' of Gateshead, and it was the only place that marriages could take place. It is unknown when the church was originally built, although historians suggest the building dates back to the 1100s and was built upon the site of a previous church that was destroyed by fire in 1080. A local historian has speculated that some of the oldest stones resemble the Roman style and could have been reclaimed from the remains of a nearby Roman building.

Despite being a place of worship, the ancient building has endured a stormy history. During the English Civil War Parliamentary soldiers were stationed at the church's rectory. The rectory was destroyed, and the church was damaged by cannon balls. In the Great Fire of 1854 the church was damaged. By 1979, the building having ceased to be used as a church, was once more ablaze; this time fire consumed the building and it was

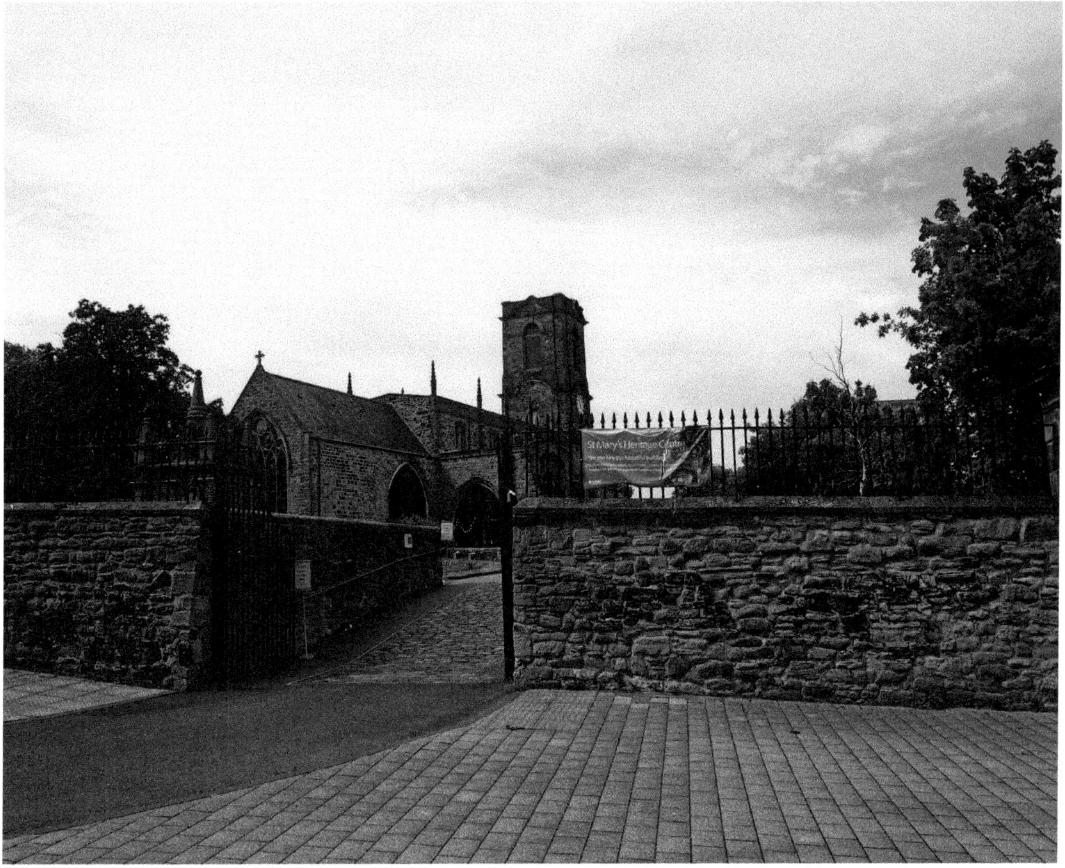

St Mary's Heritage Centre.

largely destroyed. It was rebuilt to be used as an auction room, but in 1983 the building was once again damaged by fire.

The church has barely changed over the years on the face of it; it is internally where the big changes have taken place. In a £1.2 million project funded by Gateshead Council, the European Regional Development Fund, and the Heritage Lottery Fund, the interior of the Grade I-listed church was stripped out and reopened on 16 December 2008 as St Mary's Heritage Centre – a unique visitor attraction in a stunning location on the Gateshead Quay, welcoming visitors to learning the history of Gateshead, incorporating libraries, arts and local heritage in one venue.

Bottle Bank was named for the old Saxon word '*botl*', which means 'settlement'. This street on a steep slope was once the heart of old Gateshead. In the eighteenth and early nineteenth centuries, housing and local industry centred around the steep slope of Bottle Bank and Bridge Street as they led up from the River Tyne – at the point of the only crossing of the river – at the site of the current Swing Bridge.

The importance of Bottle Bank declined in the early nineteenth century when Church Street was built, as it offered a gentler gradient. When the High Level Bridge opened in

1849 Wellington Street became the main route into Gateshead, with its bus stations and railway station.

During the 1920s much of Bottle Bank was demolished to clear land for the building of the new Tyne Bridge, which opened in 1928. More buildings were pulled down as part of the 1932–35 slum housing clearance. Over the decades that followed the rest of the former homes, businesses and public houses were destroyed. In 2001, with the rejuvenation of Gateshead's Quays taking shape, the last remaining buildings on Bottle Bank were demolished to make way for the building of a new Hilton hotel – a hugely popular hotel offering unrivalled views across the River Tyne.

A statue on the opposite side of the road from the hotel is the only reminder on the modern-day Bottle Bank of the street's heritage. It's a sculpture by north Yorkshire sculptor Peter Coates that was created in 2006 and bears the inscription 'James Hill of Bottle Bank, world renowned fiddle player and composer of tunes. The finest exponent of the Newcastle hornpipe style. Most active 1842-1852.' James Hill is considered to be one of the most talented fiddler players and tune writers of the nineteenth century. He is believed to have been born in Scotland in 1811. From the 1830s he lived on Bottle Bank near the Hawk pub with his wife Sarah, who was born in County Durham. When he composed fiddle tunes he often named them after local pubs and events in the Newcastle

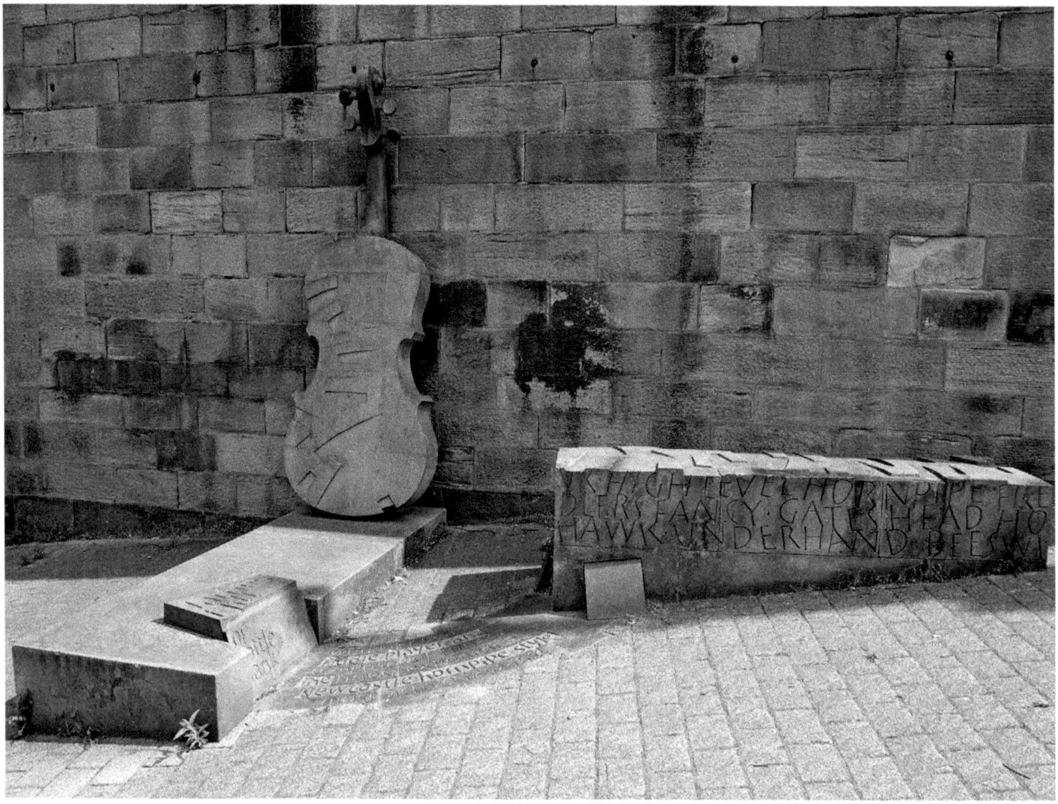

James Hill monument on Bottle Bank.

and Gateshead areas. He wrote the tune 'High Level Hornpipe' for the opening of the High Level Bridge.

In 1996 Gateshead launched a competition to find a bridge to complement the existing six bridges that cross the River Tyne from Gateshead Quays on the south bank, to the quayside of Newcastle-upon-Tyne on the north bank. Gateshead residents voted for their favourite design from over 150 entries from leading architectural companies. The chosen design would go on to win Wilkinson Eyre Architects and Gifford & Partners multiple awards. The design was for a pedestrian and cycle bridge that would 'tilt' 40 degrees to allow small ships and boats to pass underneath. It would even clean up its own litter as every time it opens anything lying on the deck of the bridge would roll into special traps at each end of the bridge.

On 20 November 2000 the bridge was lifted into place in one piece by Europe's largest floating crane, the Asian Hercules II. On 28 June 2001, 36,000 people lined the banks of the River Tyne to watch the completed Millennium Bridge tilt for the very first time, its appearance during this manoeuvre would quickly lead to it being nicknamed the 'Blinking Eye Bridge'. It would officially open for public crossing on 17 September 2001, and was dedicated by Elizabeth II on 7 May 2002.

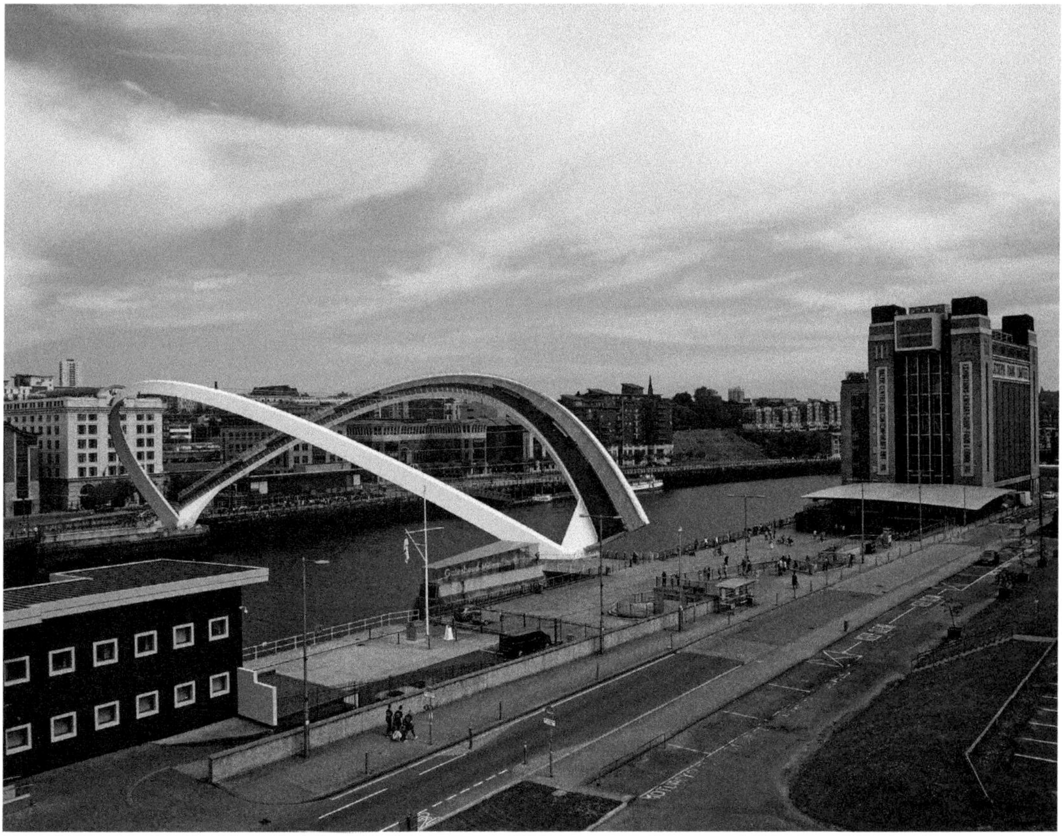

The Millennium Bridge tilted fully.

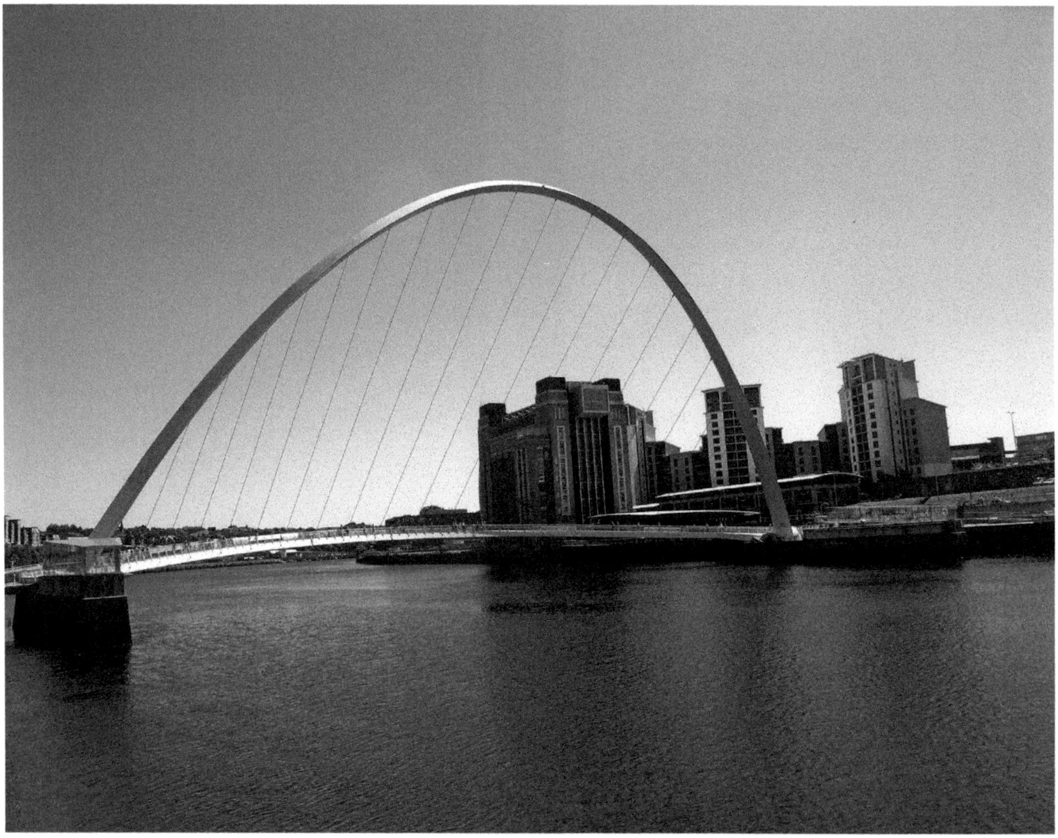

The Millennium Bridge.

Despite the bridge being relatively new, it's quickly became a Gateshead landmark, even featuring on a first-class stamp and a £1 coin. Its grace and revolutionary engineering have attracted visitors to Gateshead from all over the world.

DID YOU KNOW?

In the Baltic is an unusual piece of artwork on a staircase. There's no sign, or any explanation, as to what it is or why it's there. This art is by a French artist called Invader. In 2006, he came to Newcastle and placed his mosaic installations, influenced by 1970s video games, all over the city – without the knowledge or permission of the police. Some were also placed in Gateshead including Gateshead Metro Station, on the side of the Baltic on the Quayside side, and inside the Baltic on the staircase.

Invader's artwork would then form part of a 2006–07 exhibition of Urban Art called Spank the Monkey at the Baltic.

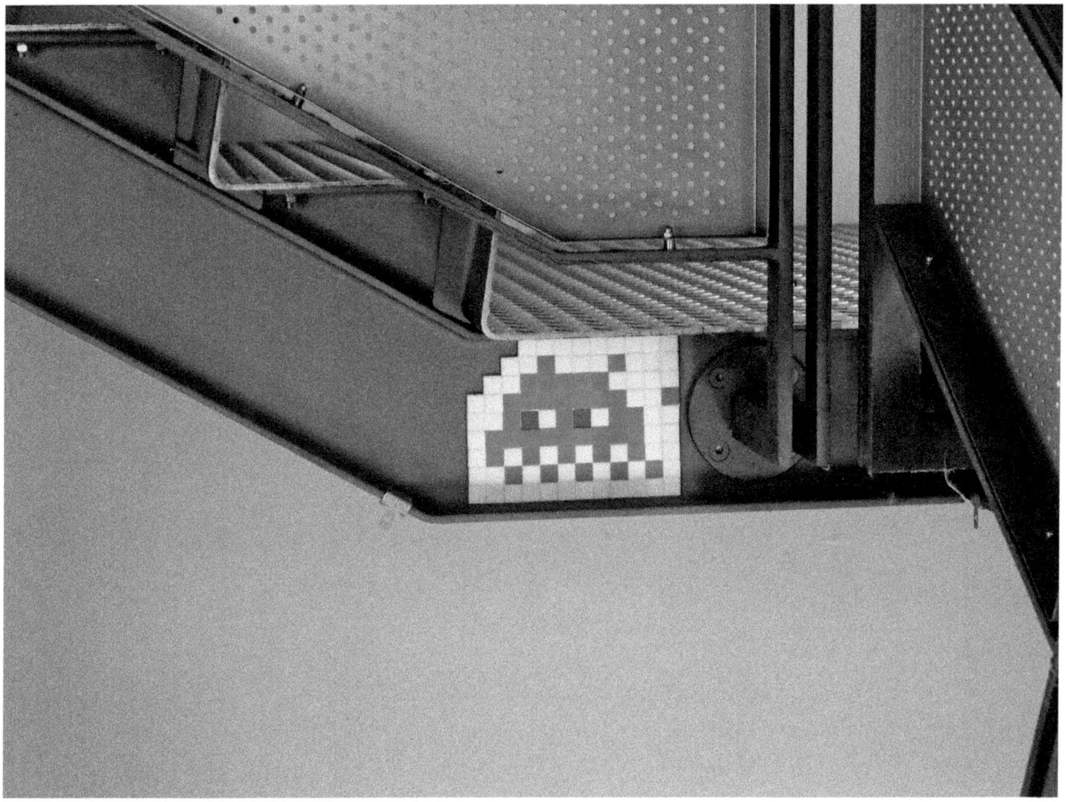

Invader in the BALTIC Centre for Contemporary Art.

The Baltic Flour Mill was designed by Hull-based architects Gelder & Kitchen for Rank Hovis in the late 1930s, to be built on the south bank of the River Tyne on the former site of the Gateshead ironworks – famous for their work on the High Level Bridge, which spans the Tyne. The foundations went up but the outbreak of the Second World War led to the project being halted. Work resumed on the mill in 1948, and it was finally completed in 1950. Even though it was built to the 1930s designs, it was equipped with the most modern machinery of the time and had a silo capacity of 22,000 tonnes and could despatch 240 tonnes of grain per hour. It was one of a number of mills located along the banks of the Tyne, all of which, due to their size, became prominent local landmarks.

At its height around 300 people were employed at the Baltic Flour Mill, with some of them moving to the area specifically to work there. In 1957 an animal food mill extension was built, and the Baltic became a dual-purpose mill; producing animal feed as well as grain.

In 1981, after only a little over thirty years in operation, and with the number of people employed at the mill down to around 100, the Baltic Flour Mill ceased production. The building remained unused and derelict for some time and the future of the industrial landmark looked uncertain. This was to change in 2002 when plans were drawn up to convert the building into an international centre for contemporary visual art.

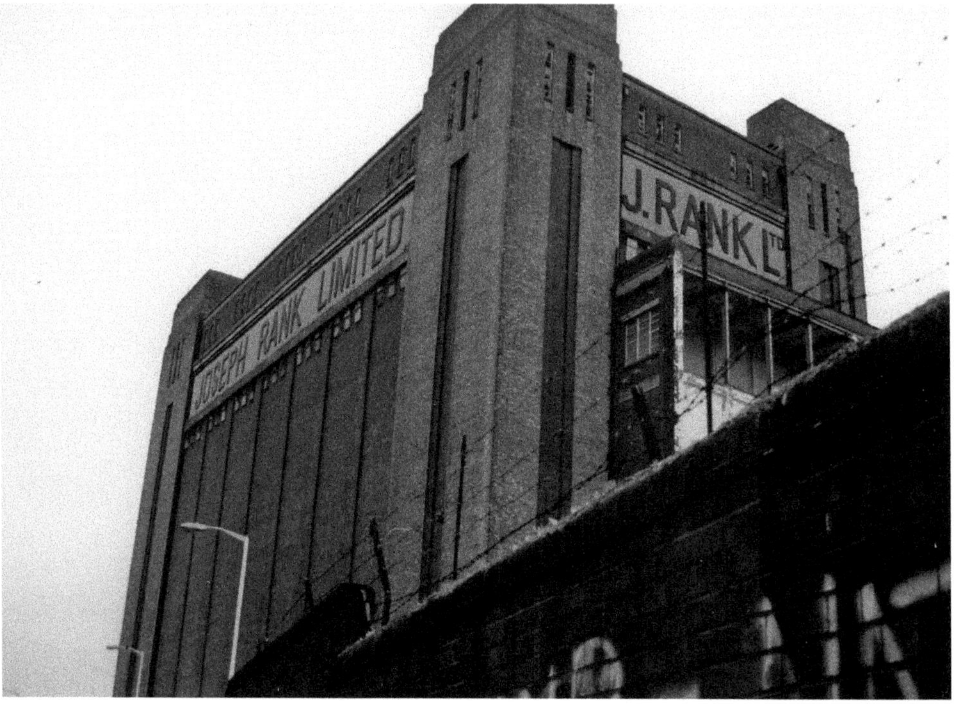

The BALTIC Centre for Contemporary Art in summer 2017. (Photo courtesy of Gateshead Libraries)

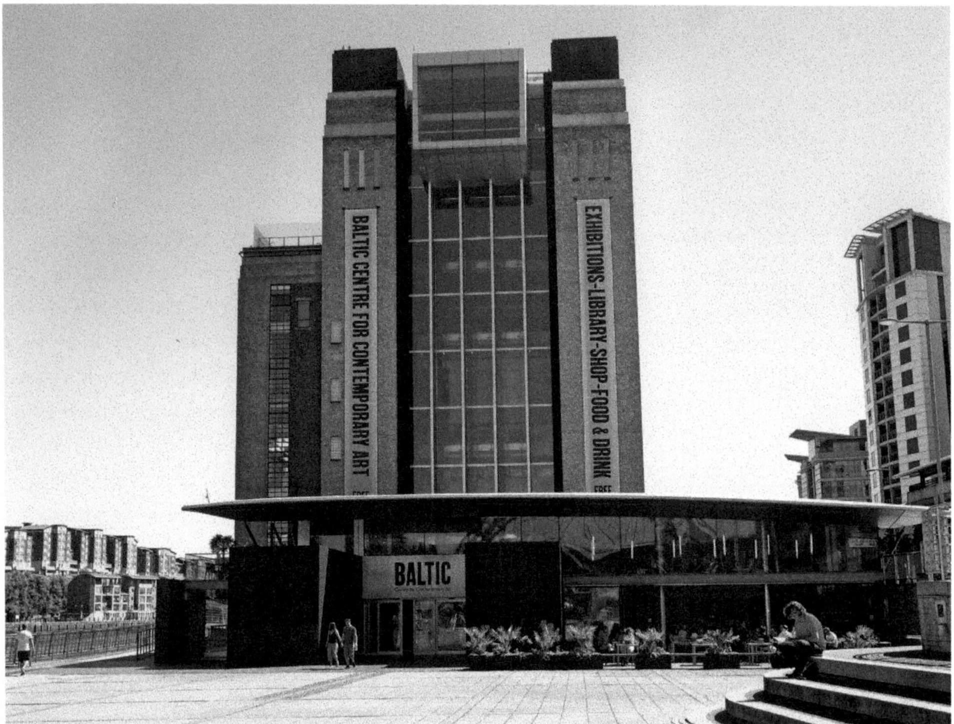

An architectural design competition was launched by Gateshead Council and the Royal Institute of British Architects, and in 1994 Dominic Williams of Ellis Williams Architects, London was announced as the winner.

Work began in 1998 on the £50 million project, which included £33.4 million from the Arts Council Lottery Fund. Only the south and north walls, and the four brick corner towers of the original 1950s building remain. A completely new interior consisted of six main floors and three mezzanines offering 3, 000 square metres of arts space, artists' studios, cinema/lecture space, shop, a library and archive for the study of contemporary art. This is topped off by a glass rooftop restaurant offering stunning panoramic views of Gateshead, Newcastle and beyond.

Baltic Centre for Contemporary Art opened to the public at midnight on Saturday 13 July 2002. The inaugural exhibition, B.OPEN, attracted over 35,000 visitors in the first week. The Baltic has proved a huge success with over 5 million visitors passing through its doors to date.

DID YOU KNOW?

Behind the Sage are a series of arches that are used for 'legal graffiti' operated as part of CoMusica's Urban Foundation Learning Programme. Artists from all over the world have come to paint the wall and the wall is open seven days a week to artists of all ages and skills. CoMusica has worked closely with local police to ensure correct and safe usage of the space and it has resulted in an 80 per cent reduction of illegal graffiti in the area.

Sage Gateshead stands on the site of the former rectory of St Mary's Church. The rectory had been described in 1834 as a 'commodius house with gardens, and commands a fine view towards the river'. It was abandoned for a new rectory in Bensham in 1839. The western part of the old rectory was taken over by Susanna Stobart and became, in stark contrast to its previous purpose, a public house called the Brandling Arms, named for the interest in the Brandling Junction construction works and the company's contribution to the industrial development of Gateshead. In 1861 the Co-operative society opened a store in the old rectory. By the late 1880s industrial development had surrounded the rectory and the building was taken over by the North East Railway. In *c.* 1914, the building was mostly pulled down and was rebuilt as offices for the Judge Brand Co. Ltd.

Sage Gateshead opened over the weekend of 17–19 December 2004 as a centre for musical education, performance and conferences. Internally it consists of three separate performance spaces insulated from one another to prevent sound and vibration travelling between them. Hall One is a 1,700-seat venue modelled on the Musikverein in Vienna and designed to be acoustically perfect. Hall Two is a unique ten-sided performance space with a seating capacity of 450, and the third building is a smaller rehearsal and performance hall.

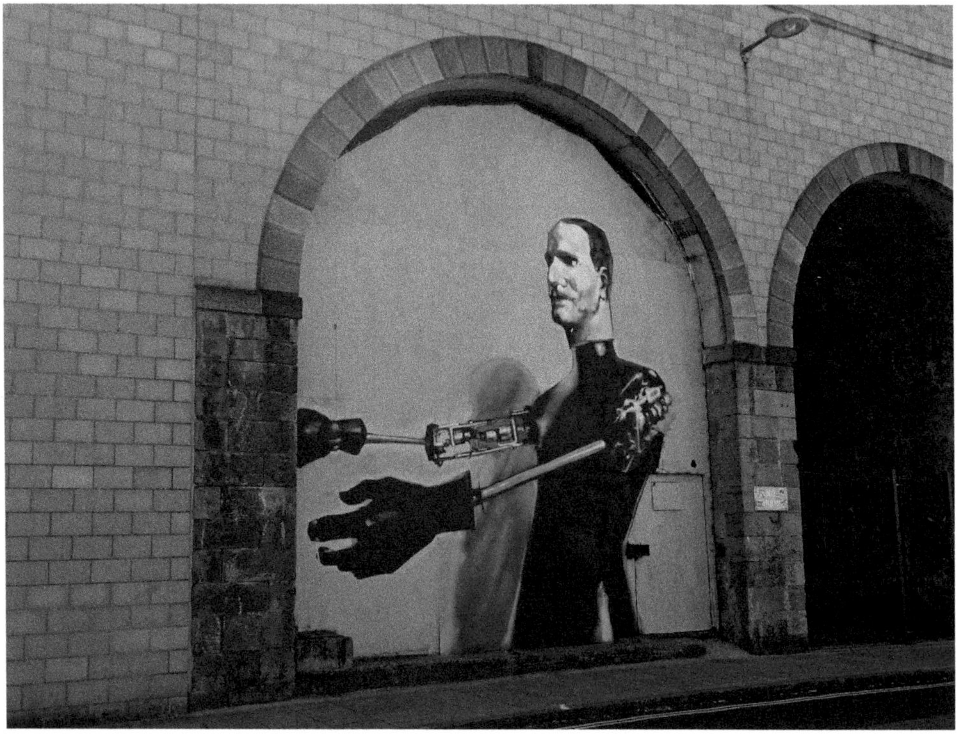

Legal graffiti.

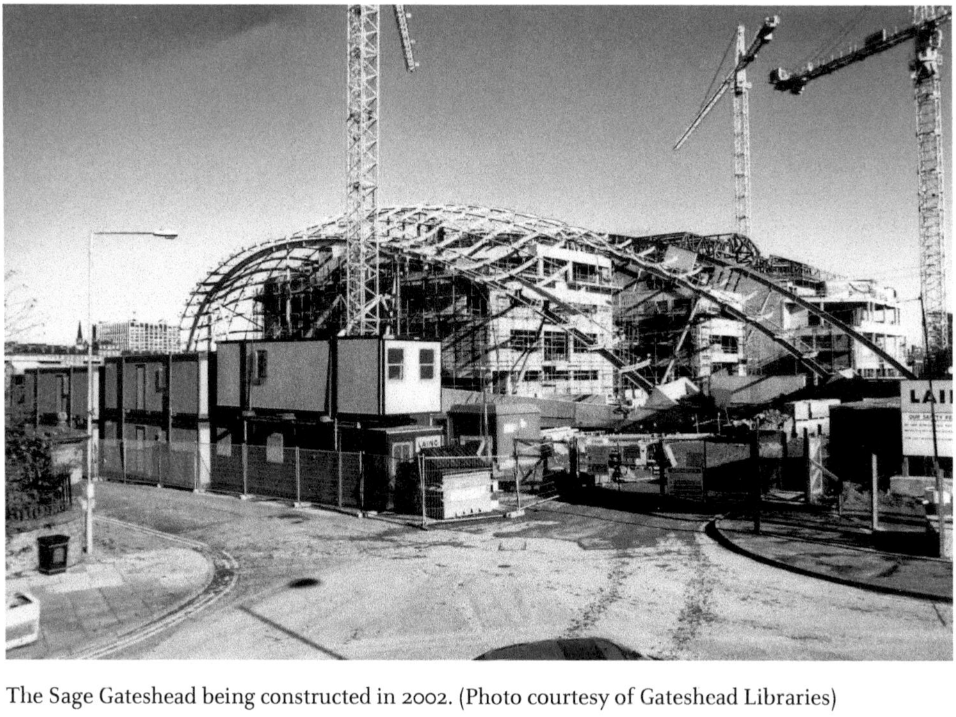

The Sage Gateshead being constructed in 2002. (Photo courtesy of Gateshead Libraries)

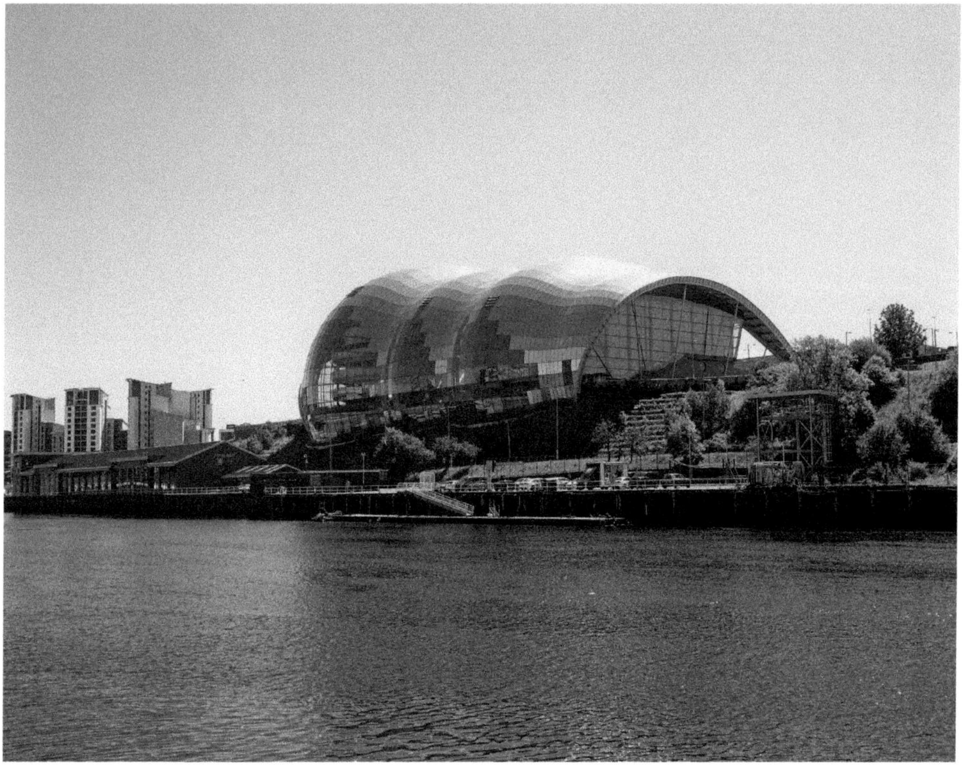

The Sage Gateshead.

The eye-catching curved glass and steel building is part of the Gateshead Quays development, which also includes the Millennium Bridge and the Baltic Centre for Contemporary Art.